Appetizers

pil
Publications International, Ltd.
Favorite Brand Name Recipes at www.fbnr.com

Louis Weber, CEO
Publications International, Ltd.
7373 North Cicero Avenue
Lincolnwood, IL 60712

Some of the products listed in this publication may be in limited distribution.

Pictured on the front cover *(clockwise from top left):* Hearty Ham Quesadillas *(page 24),* Caribbean Dream *(page 176),* Spicy Apricot Sesame Wings *(page 148)* and Cheesy Potato Skin Appetizers *(page 8).*
Pictured on the back cover *(left to right):* Easy Taco Dip *(page 110)* and Southwestern Chili Cheese Empanadas *(page 132).*

ISBN: 0-7853-9678-0

Library of Congress Control Number: 2003094512

Manufactured in China.

8 7 6 5 4 3 2 1

Microwave Cooking: Microwave ovens vary in wattage. Use the cooking times as guidelines and check for doneness before adding more time.

Preparation/Cooking Times: Preparation times are based on the approximate amount of time required to assemble the recipe before cooking, baking, chilling or serving. These times include preparation steps such as measuring, chopping and mixing. The fact that some preparations and cooking can be done simultaneously is taken into account. Preparation of optional ingredients and serving suggestions is not included.

Table of Contents

Mucho Mexican

Miniature Quesadillas

- **¼ teaspoon chili powder**
- **¼ teaspoon ground cumin**
- **¼ teaspoon salt**
- **¼ teaspoon dried oregano leaves**
- **1 cup shredded Cheddar cheese**
- **½ cup shredded Monterey Jack cheese (about 2 ounces)**
- **1½ teaspoons CRISCO® Oil**
- **4 (6-to 7-inch) flour tortillas**
- **Fresh salsa (optional)**

1. Combine chili powder, cumin, salt and oregano in large plastic food storage bag. Add Cheddar and Monterey Jack cheese. Shake to coat cheese.

2. Heat 1½ teaspoons Crisco® Oil in medium skillet. Fry one tortilla on medium-high heat 30 seconds or until golden brown. Turn, fry 30 seconds longer. Repeat with remaining tortillas.

3. Place fried tortillas on baking sheet. Sprinkle with cheese mixture. Broil 3 inches from heat 1½ to 2½ minutes, or until cheese melts. Cut each quesadilla into 4 pieces. Top with salsa, if desired. Serve hot. *Makes 4 servings*

Preparation Time: about 5 to 10 minutes
Total Time: 20 minutes

Miniature Quesadillas

Deluxe Fajita Nachos

1 tablespoon vegetable oil
4 boneless, skinless chicken breast halves (about 1 pound), thinly sliced
1 package (1.27 ounces) LAWRY'S® Spices & Seasonings for Fajitas
1/3 cup water
8 ounces tortilla chips
1 1/4 cups (5 ounces) shredded cheddar cheese
1 cup (4 ounces) shredded Monterey Jack cheese
1 large tomato, chopped
1 can (2 1/4 ounces) sliced black olives, drained
1/4 cup sliced green onions
Salsa

In medium skillet, heat oil. Add chicken and cook over medium-high heat 5 to 8 minutes. Add Spices & Seasonings for Fajitas and water; mix well. Bring to a boil over medium-high heat; reduce heat to low and simmer 7 minutes. In large shallow ovenproof platter, arrange chips. Top with chicken mixture and cheeses. Place under broiler to melt cheeses. Top with tomato, olives, green onions and desired amount of salsa.
Makes 4 appetizer or 2 main-dish servings

Serving Suggestion: Garnish with guacamole and sour cream.

Hint: For a spicier version, add sliced jalapeños.

Substitution: Substitute 1 1/4 pounds cooked ground beef in place of chicken.

Pico de Gallo

1 small jicama, peeled
3 oranges
1/4 cup lime juice
Lime wedges for garnish
Cilantro sprigs for garnish
Salt
Chili powder

Cut jicama into 3-inch matchsticks. Cut oranges in half lengthwise; cut halves crosswise into thin slices. Arrange jicama and oranges on serving plate; brush with lime juice. Garnish with lime wedges and cilantro. To serve, sprinkle with salt and chili powder to taste.
Makes 6 to 8 servings

Deluxe Fajita Nachos

Cheesy Potato Skin Appetizers

- ⅔ cup Zesty Pico De Gallo (recipe follows) or purchased salsa
- 5 potatoes (4 to 5 ounces each)
- Nonstick butter-flavor cooking spray
- 4 ounces fat-free cream cheese
- 2 tablespoons reduced-fat sour cream
- ⅓ cup shredded reduced-fat sharp Cheddar cheese
- 2 tablespoons sliced ripe olives (optional)
- ¼ cup minced fresh cilantro

1. Prepare Zesty Pico De Gallo.

2. Preheat oven to 425°F. Scrub potatoes; pierce several times with fork. Bake 45 minutes or until soft. Cool.

3. Split each potato crosswise into halves. Scoop out potato with spoon, leaving ¼-inch shell. (Reserve potato for another use). Place potato skins on baking sheet; spray lightly with cooking spray.

4. Preheat broiler. Broil potato skins 6 inches from heat, 5 minutes or until lightly brown and crisp.

5. Preheat oven to 350°F. Combine cream cheese and sour cream; stir until well blended. Divide among potato skins; spread to cover. Top with Zesty Pico De Gallo, cheese and olives, if desired. Bake 15 minutes or until heated through. Sprinkle with cilantro. *Makes 10 servings*

Zesty Pico De Gallo

- 2 cups chopped, seeded tomatoes
- 1 cup chopped green onions
- 1 can (8 ounces) tomato sauce
- ½ cup minced cilantro
- 1 to 2 tablespoons minced jalapeño peppers*
- 1 tablespoon fresh lime juice

**Jalapeño peppers can sting and irritate the skin; wear rubber gloves when handling peppers and do not touch eyes. Wash hands after handling.*

1. Combine all ingredients in medium bowl. Cover and refrigerate at least 1 hour. *Makes 4 cups*

Cheesy Potato Skin Appetizers

Grilled Chicken Tostados

1 pound boneless skinless chicken breast halves
1 teaspoon ground cumin
¼ cup orange juice
¼ cup plus 2 tablespoons salsa, divided
1 tablespoon plus 2 teaspoons vegetable oil, divided
2 cloves garlic, minced
8 green onions
1 can (16 ounces) refried beans
4 (10-inch) *or* 8 (6- to 7-inch) flour tortillas
2 cups chopped romaine lettuce
1½ cups (6 ounces) shredded Monterey Jack cheese with jalapeño peppers
1 ripe medium avocado, diced (optional)
1 medium tomato, seeded and diced (optional)
Chopped fresh cilantro and sour cream (optional)

Place chicken in single layer in shallow glass dish; sprinkle with cumin. Combine orange juice, ¼ cup salsa, 1 tablespoon oil and garlic in small bowl; pour over chicken. Cover; marinate in refrigerator at least 2 hours or up to 8 hours, stirring mixture occasionally.

Prepare grill for direct cooking.

Drain chicken; reserve marinade. Brush green onions with remaining 2 teaspoons oil. Place chicken and green onions on grid. Grill, covered, over medium-high heat 5 minutes. Brush tops of chicken with half of reserved marinade; turn and brush with remaining marinade. Turn onions. Continue to grill, covered, 5 minutes or until chicken is no longer pink in center and onions are tender. (If onions are browning too quickly, remove before chicken is done.)

Meanwhile, combine beans and remaining 2 tablespoons salsa in small saucepan; cook, stirring occasionally, over medium heat until hot.

Place tortillas in single layer on grid. Grill, uncovered, 1 to 2 minutes per side or until golden brown. (If tortillas puff up, pierce with tip of knife or flatten by pressing with spatula.)

Transfer chicken and onions to cutting board. Slice chicken crosswise into ½-inch strips. Cut onions crosswise into 1-inch-long pieces. Spread tortillas with bean mixture; top with lettuce, chicken, onions, cheese, avocado and tomato, if desired. Sprinkle with cilantro and serve with sour cream, if desired. *Makes 4 servings*

Grilled Chicken Tostada

Veggie Quesadilla Appetizers

- 10 (8-inch) flour tortillas
- 1 cup finely chopped broccoli
- 1 cup thinly sliced small mushrooms
- 3/4 cup shredded carrots
- 1/4 cup chopped green onions
- 1 1/4 cups (5 ounces) reduced-fat sharp Cheddar cheese
- 2 cups Zesty Pico De Gallo (recipe page 8)

1. Brush both sides of tortillas lightly with water. Heat small nonstick skillet over medium heat until hot. Heat tortillas, one at a time, 30 seconds on each side. Divide vegetables among 5 tortillas; sprinkle evenly with cheese. Top with remaining 5 tortillas.

2. Cook quesadillas, one at a time, in large nonstick skillet or griddle over medium heat 2 minutes on each side or until surface is crisp and cheese is melted.

3. Cut each tortilla into 4 wedges. Serve with Zesty Pico De Gallo.

Makes 20 servings

Mini Turkey Empanadas

- 1 pound ground turkey
- 1 cup chopped onion
- 1/2 cup chopped green pepper
- 1 clove garlic, minced
- 1 can (16 ounces) tomatoes, drained and crushed
- 1 tablespoon dried parsley
- 1 teaspoon dried cilantro
- 1 teaspoon cumin seed
- 1/2 teaspoon dried oregano
- 1/2 teaspoon red pepper flakes
- 1/8 teaspoon black pepper
- 2 packages (15 ounces each) refrigerated pie crusts
- Nonstick cooking spray

1. In large nonstick skillet, over medium-high heat, sauté turkey, onion, green pepper and garlic 5 to 6 minutes or until turkey is no longer pink and vegetables are tender. Stir in tomatoes, parsley, cilantro, cumin, oregano, pepper flakes and black pepper. Reduce heat to medium and cook 10 to 15 minutes, stirring constantly, or until any liquid is evaporated. Remove skillet from heat and cool.

2. Using 3-inch round biscuit cutter, cut 12 rounds from each pie crust, combining remaining crust to yield 48 rounds.

3. Spoon heaping teaspoonful of filling in center of each round. Fold each pastry in half and pinch edges together to seal. Place mini empanadas on two 15×10-inch cookie sheets lightly coated with nonstick cooking spray. Bake at 400°F 15 to 20 minutes or until mini empanadas are golden brown.

Makes 48 empanadas

Favorite recipe from **National Turkey Federation**

Veggie Quesadilla Appetizers

Carnitas

2 to 2½ pounds pork butt
2 bay leaves
2 cloves garlic, minced
1 teaspoon chili powder
¾ teaspoon salt
½ teaspoon black pepper
½ teaspoon dried oregano
½ teaspoon ground cumin
½ cup water
Guacamole (recipe follows) *or* 2 cups salsa

Preheat oven to 350°F. Trim external fat from meat; cut meat into 1-inch cubes. Combine bay leaves, garlic, chili powder, salt, pepper, oregano and cumin in large shallow roasting pan (pan should be large enough to hold meat in single layer). Gradually add water; mix well. Place meat in pan; stir until well coated. Cover with foil. Bake 45 minutes. Remove foil; continue baking 45 to 60 minutes or until most of the liquid has evaporated and meat begins to brown. Discard bay leaves. Transfer meat to fondue pot or chafing dish; keep warm over heat source. Serve with Guacamole.

Makes 12 to 14 servings

Guacamole

2 large avocados, peeled and pitted
¼ cup finely chopped tomato
2 tablespoons lime juice or lemon juice
2 tablespoons grated onion with juice
½ teaspoon salt
¼ teaspoon hot pepper sauce
Black pepper

Place avocados in medium bowl; mash coarsely with fork. Stir in tomato, lime juice, onion, salt and pepper sauce; mix well. Add black pepper to taste. Spoon into serving container. Serve immediately or cover and refrigerate up to 2 hours. Garnish with additional chopped tomatoes, if desired.

Makes 2 cups

Guacamole

Hearty Nachos

1 pound ground beef
1 envelope LIPTON® RECIPE SECRETS® Onion Soup Mix
1 can (19 ounces) black beans, rinsed and drained
1 cup prepared salsa
1 package (8½ ounces) plain tortilla chips
1 cup shredded Cheddar cheese (about 4 ounces)

1. In 12-inch nonstick skillet, brown ground beef over medium-high heat; drain.

2. Stir in soup mix, black beans and salsa. Bring to a boil over high heat. Reduce heat to low and simmer 5 minutes or until heated through.

3. Arrange tortilla chips on serving platter. Spread beef mixture over chips; sprinkle with Cheddar cheese. Top, if desired, with sliced green onions, sliced pitted ripe olives, chopped tomato and chopped cilantro. *Makes 8 servings*

Prep Time: 10 minutes
Cook Time: 12 minutes

Bean Tortilla Pinwheels

8 corn tortillas (6 inches each)
1 cup GUILTLESS GOURMET® Black Bean Dip (Spicy or Mild)

To soften tortillas, stack 4 tortillas and wrap in damp paper towel. Microwave on HIGH (100% power) 20 seconds. Or, to soften tortillas in oven, preheat oven to 300°F. Wrap tortillas in foil. Bake 10 minutes.

Spread 2 tablespoons bean dip on each tortilla and roll up tightly. Evenly place toothpicks through rolls, using 6 toothpicks per tortilla. Carefully cut between toothpicks to maintain round shape and obtain 6 pinwheels per tortilla. Serve immediately.

Makes 48 pinwheels

Hearty Nachos

Chili con Queso

1 pound pasteurized process cheese spread, cut into cubes
1 can (10 ounces) diced tomatoes with green chilies, undrained
1 cup sliced green onions
2 teaspoons ground coriander
2 teaspoons ground cumin
¾ teaspoon hot pepper sauce
Green onion strips (optional)
Hot pepper slices (optional)

Slow Cooker Directions

Combine all ingredients except green onion strips and hot pepper slices in slow cooker until well blended. Cover and cook on LOW 2 to 3 hours or until hot.* Garnish with green onion strips and hot pepper slices, if desired. *Makes 3 cups*

**Chili will be very hot; use caution when serving.*

Serving Suggestion: Serve Chili con Queso with tortilla chips. Or, for something different, cut pita bread into triangles and toast in preheated 400°F oven for 5 minutes or until crisp.

Ranch-Style Crab Caliente

1 package (8 ounces) cream cheese, softened
1 cup mayonnaise
1 packet (.4 ounce) HIDDEN VALLEY® The Original Ranch® Buttermilk Recipe Salad Dressing Mix
2 tablespoons lemon juice
1 large tomato, seeded and chopped
½ cup chopped green onions
6 ounces fresh or canned crabmeat
1 tablespoon diced seeded jalapeño pepper
Parsley and paprika

Preheat oven to 350°F. In medium bowl, blend cream cheese, mayonnaise, salad dressing mix and lemon juice until smooth. Stir in tomato, green onions, crabmeat and jalapeño. Spoon mixture into small casserole dish; bake 15 minutes. Remove from oven, garnish with parsley and lightly dust surface with paprika. Serve immediately with fresh bread or crackers.

Makes 8 to 10 servings

Chili con Queso

Mexican Roll-Ups

- 6 uncooked lasagna noodles
- ¾ cup prepared guacamole
- ¾ cup chunky salsa
- ¾ cup (3 ounces) shredded fat-free Cheddar cheese
- Additional salsa (optional)

1. Cook lasagna noodles according to package directions, omitting salt. Rinse with cool water; drain. Cool.

2. Spread 2 tablespoons guacamole onto each noodle; top each with 2 tablespoons salsa and 2 tablespoons cheese.

3. Roll up noodles jelly-roll fashion. Cut each roll-up in half to form two equal-size roll-ups. Serve immediately with salsa or cover with plastic wrap and refrigerate up to 3 hours.

Makes 12 appetizers

Health Note: Ten percent of the sodium in American diets comes from natural foods, 75 percent comes from processed and canned goods, and the remaining 15 percent is added during cooking or at the table.

Fajitas Festivas

- 1 pound boneless, skinless chicken breast, cut in 1×1½-inch strips
- 1 cup chunky salsa mild
- ¼ cup Italian salad dressing
- ¼ cup chopped fresh cilantro (optional)
- 1 tablespoon lemon juice
- ½ teaspoon garlic powder
- 2 tablespoons WESSON® Vegetable Oil, divided
- 1 cup each: bell pepper strips and thin onion strips
- 1 (16-ounce) can ROSARITA® Refried Beans
- Flour tortillas, warmed
- Shredded Cheddar cheese (optional)
- Guacamole (optional)

In shallow bowl, mix together first 6 ingredients. Cover and refrigerate 2 to 4 hours to marinate. Drain chicken; discard marinade. In large skillet, heat 1 Tablespoon oil and saute half of chicken in oil until chicken is no longer pink. Add half of bell pepper and onion. Continue cooking 1 to 3 minutes or until vegetables are crisp-tender; remove from skillet. Repeat with remaining oil, chicken, bell pepper and onion. Serve immediately with refried beans and tortillas. If desired, serve with additional salsa or top with cheese and guacamole.

Makes 8 fajitas

Mexican Roll-Ups

Cheesy Chorizo Wedges

Red & Green Salsa (recipe follows, optional)
8 ounces chorizo
1 cup (4 ounces) shredded mild Cheddar cheese
1 cup (4 ounces) shredded Monterey Jack cheese
3 flour tortillas (10-inch diameter)

1. Prepare Red & Green Salsa.

2. Remove and discard casing from chorizo. Heat medium skillet over high heat until hot. Reduce heat to medium. Crumble chorizo into skillet. Brown 6 to 8 minutes, stirring to separate meat. Remove with slotted spoon; drain on paper towels.

3. Preheat oven to 450°F. Combine cheeses in small bowl.

4. Place tortillas on baking sheets. Divide chorizo evenly among tortillas, leaving ½ inch of edges of tortillas uncovered. Sprinkle cheese mixture over top.

5. Bake 8 to 10 minutes until edges are crisp and golden and cheese is bubbly and melted.

6. Transfer to serving plates; cut each tortilla into 6 wedges. Sprinkle Red & Green Salsa on wedges, if desired.

Makes 6 to 8 servings

Red & Green Salsa

1 small red bell pepper
¼ cup coarsely chopped fresh cilantro
3 green onions, cut into thin slices
2 fresh jalapeño peppers,* seeded, minced
2 tablespoons fresh lime juice
1 clove garlic, minced
¼ teaspoon salt

**Jalapeño peppers can sting and irritate the skin; wear rubber gloves when handling peppers and do not touch eyes. Wash hands after handling.*

1. Cut bell pepper lengthwise in half; remove and discard seeds and veins. Cut halves lengthwise into thin slivers; cut slivers crosswise into halves.

2. Mix all ingredients in small bowl. Let stand, covered, at room temperature 1 to 2 hours to blend flavors.

Makes 1 cup

Cheesy Chorizo Wedges

Hearty Ham Quesadillas

1 pound HILLSHIRE FARM® Ham, chopped
1 cup reduced-fat Monterey Jack cheese
¼ cup minced onion
1 to 2 jalapeño peppers, seeded and minced
4 tablespoons minced cilantro
½ teaspoon black pepper
¼ teaspoon salt
8 (10-inch) flour tortillas
Prepared tomato salsa

Preheat oven to 500°F.

Combine Ham, cheese, onion, jalapeño pepper, cilantro, black pepper and salt in large bowl. Arrange ⅛ of ham mixture on each tortilla, covering ½ of tortilla. Fold each tortilla over to make half-moons.

Place tortillas in shallow baking pan. Bake until tortillas are crisp and golden, about 5 minutes. Cut into wedges; serve with salsa.

Makes 8 servings

Taco Chicken Nachos

2 small boneless skinless chicken breasts (about 8 ounces)
1 tablespoon plus 1½ teaspoons taco seasoning mix
1 teaspoon olive oil
¾ cup fat-free sour cream
1 can (4 ounces) chopped mild green chilies, drained
¼ cup minced red onion
1 bag (8 ounces) baked fat-free tortilla chips
1 cup (4 ounces) shredded reduced-fat Cheddar or Monterey Jack cheese
½ cup chopped tomato
¼ cup pitted ripe olive slices (optional)
2 tablespoons chopped fresh cilantro (optional)

1. Bring 2 cups water to a boil in small saucepan. Add chicken. Reduce heat to low; cover. Simmer 10 minutes or until chicken is no longer pink in center. Remove from saucepan; cool. Chop chicken.

2. Combine taco seasoning mix and oil in small bowl; mix until smooth paste forms. Stir in sour cream. Add chicken, green chilies and onion; mix lightly.

3. Preheat broiler. Arrange tortilla chips on small ovenproof plates or large platter; cover chips with chicken mixture and cheese. Broil 4 inches from heat 2 to 3 minutes or until chicken mixture is hot and cheese is melted. Sprinkle evenly with tomato, olives, and cilantro, if desired, Serve hot.

Makes 12 servings

Hearty Ham Quesadillas

Chili Chip Party Platter

- 1 pound ground beef
- 1 medium onion, chopped
- 1 package (1.48 ounces) LAWRY'S® Spices & Seasonings for Chili
- 1 can (6 ounces) tomato paste
- 1 cup water
- 1 bag (8 to 9 ounces) tortilla chips or corn chips
- 1½ cups (6 ounces) shredded cheddar cheese
- 1 can (2¼ ounces) sliced pitted black olives, drained
- ½ cup sliced green onions

In medium skillet, cook ground beef until browned and crumbly; drain fat. Add onion, Spices & Seasonings for Chili, tomato paste and water; mix well. Bring to a boil over medium-high heat; reduce heat to low and simmer, uncovered, 15 minutes, stirring occasionally. Serve over tortilla chips. Top with cheddar cheese, olives and green onions.

Makes 4 servings

Serving Suggestion: Serve with a cool beverage and sliced melon.

Fiesta Quesadillas with Fruit Salsa

- 1 can (11 ounces) DOLE® Mandarin Oranges, drained and finely chopped
- 1 tablespoon chopped fresh cilantro or fresh parsley
- 1 tablespoon lime juice
- 4 (8-inch) whole wheat or flour tortillas
- ¾ cup shredded low fat Monterey Jack, mozzarella or Cheddar cheese
- ⅔ cup finely chopped DOLE® Pitted Dates or Chopped Dates or finely chopped Pitted Prunes
- ⅓ cup crumbled feta cheese
- 2 tablespoons chopped green onion

• Combine mandarin oranges, cilantro and lime juice in small bowl for salsa; set aside.

• Place two tortillas on large baking sheet. Sprinkle half of shredded cheese, dates, feta and green onion over each tortilla to within ½ inch of edge.

• Brush outer ½-inch edge of each tortilla with water. Top with remaining tortillas; press down edges gently to seal.

• Bake at 375°F 5 to 8 minutes or until hot. Cut each quesadilla into 6 wedges.

• Drain salsa just before serving, if desired; serve over warm quesadillas.

Makes 6 servings

Prep Time: 15 minutes
Bake Time: 8 minutes

Chili Chip Party Platter

Tiny Seafood Tostadas with Black Bean Dip

- Nonstick cooking spray
- 4 (8-inch) whole wheat or flour tortillas, cut into 32 ($2^1/_2$-inch) rounds or shapes
- 1 cup Black Bean Dip (recipe follows)
- 1 cup shredded fresh spinach
- $^3/_4$ cup tiny cooked or canned shrimp
- $^3/_4$ cup salsa
- $^1/_2$ cup (2 ounces) shredded reduced-fat Monterey Jack cheese
- $^1/_4$ cup light sour cream

Preheat oven to 350°F. Spray cooking spray on baking sheet. Place tortilla rounds evenly on prepared baking sheet. Lightly spray tortilla rounds with cooking spray and bake 10 minutes. Turn over and spray again; bake 3 minutes more. Meanwhile, prepare Black Bean Dip.

To prepare tostadas, spread each toasted tortilla round with $1^1/_2$ teaspoons Black Bean Dip. Layer each with $1^1/_2$ teaspoons shredded spinach, 1 teaspoon shrimp, 1 teaspoon salsa, a sprinkle of cheese and a dab of sour cream. Garnish with thin green chili strips or fresh cilantro, if desired. Serve immediately.

Makes 8 appetizer servings

Black Bean Dip

- 1 can (15 ounces) black beans, undrained
- 1 teaspoon chili powder
- $^1/_4$ teaspoon salt
- $^1/_4$ teaspoon black pepper
- $^1/_4$ teaspoon ground cumin
- 2 drops hot pepper sauce
- $^3/_4$ cup minced white onion
- 2 cloves garlic, minced
- 1 can (4 ounces) chopped green chilies, drained

Drain beans, reserving 2 tablespoons liquid. Combine drained beans, reserved liquid, chili powder, salt, black pepper, cumin and hot pepper sauce in blender or food processor; process until smooth.

Combine onion and garlic in nonstick skillet or saucepan; cover and cook over low heat until onion is soft and translucent. Uncover and cook until slightly browned. Add chilies and cook 3 minutes more. Add bean mixture and mix well.

Makes about $1^1/_2$ cups

Note: Black Bean Dip can be served (hot or cold) as a dip for tortilla chips or cut-up fresh vegetables.

Tiny Seafood Tostadas with Black Bean Dip

Grilled Quesadilla Snacks

- 1½ cups (6 ounces) shredded Monterey Jack cheese
- ½ red or yellow bell pepper, chopped
- 2 ounces sliced smoked ham, cut into thin strips
- 2 ounces sliced smoked turkey, cut into thin strips
- ¼ cup finely chopped green onions
- ⅓ cup *French's*® Classic Yellow® Mustard
- 2 teaspoons ground cumin
- 10 flour tortillas (6 inch)

1. Combine cheese, bell pepper, ham, turkey and onions in medium bowl. Combine mustard and cumin in small bowl; mix well.

2. Place 5 tortillas on sheet of waxed paper. Spread 1 rounded teaspoon mustard mixture over each tortilla. Sprinkle cheese mixture evenly over mustard mixture. Top with another tortilla, pressing down firmly to form quesadilla.

3. Place quesadillas on oiled grid. Grill over medium heat 2 minutes or until cheese is melted and heated through, turning once. Cut each quesadilla into quarters. Serve with salsa and cilantro, if desired.

Makes 10 servings

Prep Time: 30 minutes
Cook Time: 2 minutes

Spicy Pork Quesadillas

- ½ pound lean ground pork
- ¼ cup diced onion
- 1 clove garlic, minced
- ¼ cup chopped fresh cilantro leaves
- ¼ teaspoon ground cumin
- ¼ teaspoon dried oregano leaves, crushed
- ½ jalapeño pepper, minced
- 4 (10-inch) flour tortillas
- 4 tablespoons shredded Cheddar or Monterey Jack cheese

In large nonstick skillet over medium-high heat, cook pork, onion and garlic until browned; drain off any drippings and remove to large bowl. Stir cilantro, cumin, oregano and jalapeño into pork mixture. Wipe out skillet with paper towel and heat over medium-high heat. Place 1 tortilla in skillet; top with half the pork mixture, spreading evenly. Sprinkle with 2 tablespoons cheese. Top with another tortilla and cook 2 to 3 minutes or until browned, pressing down occasionally on top tortilla. Turn and brown other side; remove to cutting board and cut into 8 wedges. Repeat with remaining ingredients to make 8 more quesadilla wedges. Serve with salsa, if desired.

Makes 16 servings

Prep Time: 20 minutes

Favorite recipe from **National Pork Board**

Grilled Quesadilla Snacks

Classic Guacamole

4 tablespoons finely chopped white onion, divided
1 tablespoon plus 1½ teaspoons coarsely chopped fresh cilantro, divided
1 or 2 fresh serrano or jalapeño peppers,* seeded and finely chopped
¼ teaspoon chopped garlic (optional)
2 large soft avocados
1 medium tomato, peeled and chopped
1 to 2 teaspoons fresh lime juice
¼ teaspoon salt
Corn Tortilla Chips (recipe follows) or packaged corn tortilla chips
Chilies and cilantro sprig for garnish

**Serrano and jalapeño peppers can sting and irritate the skin; wear rubber gloves when handling peppers and do not touch eyes. Wash hands after handling.*

1. Combine 2 tablespoons onion, 1 tablespoon cilantro, peppers and garlic, if desired, in large mortar. Grind with pestle until almost smooth. (Mixture can be processed in blender, if necessary, but it will become more watery than desired.)

2. Cut avocados lengthwise into halves; remove and discard pits. Scoop out avocado flesh; place in bowl. Add pepper mixture. Mash roughly, leaving avocado slightly chunky.

3. Add tomato, lime juice, salt and remaining 2 tablespoons onion and 1½ teaspoons cilantro to avocado mixture; mix well. Serve immediately or cover and refrigerate up to 4 hours. Serve with Corn Tortilla Chips. Garnish, if desired.

Makes about 2 cups

Corn Tortilla Chips

12 corn tortillas (6-inch diameter), day-old**
Vegetable oil
½ to 1 teaspoon salt

***If tortillas are fresh, let stand, uncovered, in single layer on wire rack 1 to 2 hours to dry slightly.*

1. Stack 6 tortillas. Cutting through stack, cut tortillas into 6 or 8 equal wedges. Repeat with remaining tortillas.

2. Heat ½ inch oil in deep, heavy, large skillet over medium-high heat to 375°F; adjust heat to maintain temperature.

3. Fry tortilla wedges in single layer 1 minute or until crisp, turning occasionally. Remove and drain on paper towels. Repeat until all chips have been fried. Sprinkle chips with salt.

Makes 6 to 8 dozen chips

Note: Tortilla chips are served with salsa as a snack, used as the base for nachos and used as scoops for guacamole, other dips or refried beans. They are best eaten fresh, but can be stored, tightly covered, in cool place 2 or 3 days. Reheat in 350°F oven a few minutes before serving.

Classic Guacamole

Avocados with Tomato Relish

1 tablespoon cider vinegar
1 tablespoon fresh orange juice
1 teaspoon grated orange peel
¼ teaspoon salt
Dash black pepper
3 tablespoons olive oil
3 fresh plum tomatoes (about ½ pound)
¼ cup coarsely chopped fresh cilantro
2 tablespoons finely chopped mild red onion
1 fresh jalapeño pepper,* seeded and finely chopped
2 large, firm ripe avocados
2 cups shredded iceberg lettuce
Cilantro sprig, orange peel and tomato slice for garnish

**Jalapeño peppers can sting and irritate the skin; wear rubber gloves when handling peppers and do not touch eyes. Wash hands after handling.*

1. Mix vinegar, orange juice, orange peel, salt and black pepper in medium bowl. Gradually add oil, whisking continuously, until dressing is thoroughly blended.

2. Add tomatoes, chopped cilantro, onion and jalapeño pepper to dressing; toss lightly to mix. Let stand, covered, at room temperature up to 2 hours to blend flavors.

3. Just before serving, cut avocados lengthwise into halves; remove and discard pits. Pare avocados and cut lengthwise into ½-inch-thick slices.

4. Arrange avocados over lettuce-lined plates; top with tomato relish. Garnish, if desired. *Makes 4 servings*

Creamy Corn Salsa

1 cup frozen whole kernel corn, thawed and drained
¼ cup milk
2 tablespoons *Frank's® RedHot®* Cayenne Pepper Sauce
2 tablespoons chopped fresh cilantro

Combine corn, milk and ***Frank's RedHot*** Sauce in blender or food processor. Cover; process until puréed. Pour into small saucepan. Stir in cilantro. Cook over medium heat until heated through, stirring often. *Makes 1 cup salsa*

Avocados with Tomato Relish

Garden Fresh Gazpacho

4 large tomatoes (about 2 pounds)
1 large cucumber, peeled and seeded
½ red bell pepper, seeded
½ green bell pepper, seeded
½ red onion
3 cloves garlic
¼ cup *Frank's® RedHot®* Cayenne Pepper Sauce
¼ cup red wine vinegar
3 tablespoons olive oil
2 tablespoons minced fresh basil
1 teaspoon salt
Additional 2 cups chopped mixed fresh vegetables, such as tomatoes, bell peppers, cucumbers and green onions

1. Coarsely chop 4 tomatoes, 1 cucumber, ½ red bell pepper, ½ green bell pepper, ½ red onion and garlic; place in food processor or blender. Add ***Frank's RedHot*** Sauce, vinegar, oil, basil and salt. Cover; process until very smooth. (Process in batches if necessary.) Transfer soup to large glass serving bowl.

2. Stir in additional chopped vegetables, leaving some for garnish, if desired. Cover; refrigerate 1 hour before serving.

Makes 6 servings (6 cups)

Nachos Supremos

½ of a 10-ounce bag tortilla chips
1 package (8 ounces) pasteurized process cheese with jalapeño peppers, cut into ½-inch cubes
1 cup (4 ounces) shredded Monterey Jack cheese
1⅓ cups *French's®* French Fried Onions
Chopped fresh tomatoes
Sliced ripe olives

Layer chips, cheeses and French Fried Onions on large microwavable dish. Microwave on HIGH 2 to 3 minutes or until cheeses melt. Top with tomatoes and olives.

Makes 4 servings

Prep Time: 5 minutes
Cook Time: 2 minutes

Garden Fresh Gazpacho

Bite Size Tacos

1 pound ground beef
1 package (1.25 ounces) taco seasoning mix
2 cups *French's*® French Fried Onions, divided
¼ cup chopped fresh cilantro
32 bite-size round tortilla chips
¾ cup sour cream
1 cup shredded Cheddar cheese

1. Cook beef in nonstick skillet over medium-high heat 5 minutes or until browned; drain. Stir in taco seasoning mix, *¾ cup water, 1 cup* French Fried Onions and cilantro. Simmer 5 minutes or until flavors are blended, stirring often.

2. Preheat oven to 350°F. Arrange tortilla chips on foil-lined baking sheet. Top with beef mixture, sour cream, remaining onions and cheese.

3. Bake 5 minutes or until cheese is melted and onions are golden. *Makes 8 appetizer servings*

Prep Time: 5 minutes
Cook Time: 15 minutes

Rio Grande Quesadillas

2 cups shredded cooked chicken
1 package (1.0 ounce) LAWRY'S® Taco Spices & Seasonings
¾ cup water
1 can (16 ounces) refried beans
6 large flour tortillas
1½ cups (6 ounces) shredded Monterey Jack cheese
¼ cup chopped pimiento
¼ cup chopped green onions
¼ cup chopped fresh cilantro
Vegetable oil or cooking spray

In medium skillet, combine chicken, Taco Spices & Seasonings and water. Bring to a boil over medium-high heat; reduce heat to low and simmer, uncovered, 15 minutes. Stir in refried beans. Spread approximately ⅓ cup chicken-bean mixture over half of each tortilla. Top each with equal portions of cheese, pimiento, green onions and cilantro. Fold each tortilla in half. In large skillet, heat small amount of oil or spray skillet and heat over medium-high heat until hot. Quickly cook each quesadilla until slightly crisp, turning once. *Makes 6 servings*

Serving Suggestion: Cut each quesadilla into quarters; serve with chunky salsa and guacamole.

Bite Size Tacos

Black Bean Cakes with Salsa Cruda

- Salsa Cruda (recipe follows)
- 1 can (about 15 ounces) black beans, rinsed and drained
- ¼ cup all-purpose flour
- ¼ cup chopped fresh cilantro
- 2 tablespoons plain low-fat yogurt
- 1 tablespoon chili powder
- 2 cloves garlic, minced
- Nonstick cooking spray

Prepare Salsa Cruda; set aside. Place beans in medium bowl; mash with fork or potato masher until almost smooth, leaving some beans in larger pieces. Stir in flour, cilantro, yogurt, chili powder and garlic.

Spray large nonstick skillet with cooking spray; heat over medium-high heat until hot. For each cake, drop 2 heaping tablespoonfuls bean mixture onto bottom of skillet; flatten to form cake with back of spoon. Cook 6 to 8 minutes or until lightly browned, turning once. Serve with Salsa Cruda. Garnish as desired. *Makes 4 servings*

Salsa Cruda

- 1 cup chopped seeded tomato
- 2 tablespoons minced onion
- 2 tablespoons minced fresh cilantro (optional)
- 2 tablespoons lime juice
- ½ jalapeño pepper,* seeded and minced
- 1 clove garlic, minced

**Jalapeño peppers can sting and irritate the skin. Wear rubber gloves when handling peppers and do not touch eyes. Wash hands after handling.*

Combine all ingredients in small bowl. Refrigerate 1 hour before serving. *Makes 4 servings*

Black Bean Cakes with Salsa Cruda

Molletes

Butter or margarine
8 to 10 French rolls, cut lengthwise into halves or quarters
LAWRY'S® Garlic Powder with Parsley
1 can (16 ounces) refried beans
Salsa
2 cups (8 ounces) shredded cheddar or Monterey Jack cheese

Spread butter on cut sides of rolls; lightly sprinkle with Garlic Powder with Parsley. Toast under broiler until just golden. Spread each with equally divided portions of refried beans and salsa. Top with cheese. Broil until heated through and cheese is melted. *Makes 16 to 20 appetizers*

Serving Suggestion: Serve with guacamole.

Layered Mexican Dip

1 package (8 ounces) cream cheese, softened
1 tablespoon plus 1 teaspoon taco seasoning mix
1 cup canned black beans
1 cup salsa
1 cup shredded lettuce
1 cup (4 ounces) shredded Cheddar cheese
½ cup chopped green onions
2 tablespoons sliced pitted ripe olives
Tortilla chips

Combine cream cheese and seasoning mix in small bowl. Spread on bottom of 9-inch pie plate.

Layer remaining ingredients over cream cheese mixture. Refrigerate until ready to serve. Serve with tortilla chips. *Makes 10 servings*

Prep time: 10 minutes plus refrigerating

Molletes

Island Oasis

Coconut-Orange Shrimp

- **2½ cups flaked coconut, divided**
- **1 medium ripe banana**
- **¼ cup *Frank's® RedHot®* Cayenne Pepper Sauce**
- **¼ cup orange juice**
- **1 tablespoon olive oil**
- **1 tablespoon grated orange peel**
- **1 pound raw large shrimp, shelled and deveined**

1. Combine ½ cup coconut, banana, ***Frank's RedHot*** Sauce, juice, oil and orange peel in blender or food processor; process until puréed.

2. Pour into resealable plastic food storage bag. Add shrimp; toss to coat. Seal bag. Refrigerate 1 hour.

3. Preheat oven to 450°F. Line baking pan with foil; grease foil. Sprinkle remaining coconut onto sheet of waxed paper. Dip shrimp into coconut, pressing firmly to coat. (Do not shake off excess marinade from shrimp.) Place shrimp on prepared baking pan. Bake 6 to 8 minutes or until shrimp are opaque.

Makes 6 servings

Prep Time: 30 minutes
Marinate Time: 1 hour
Cook Time: 6 minutes

Coconut-Orange Shrimp

Caribbean Chutney Kabobs

20 (4-inch) bamboo skewers
½ medium pineapple
1 medium red bell pepper, cut into 1-inch pieces
¾ pound boneless skinless chicken breasts, cut into 1-inch pieces
½ cup bottled mango chutney
2 tablespoons orange juice or pineapple juice
1 teaspoon vanilla
¼ teaspoon ground nutmeg

1. To prevent burning, soak skewers in water at least 20 minutes before assembling kabobs.

2. Peel and core pineapple. Cut pineapple into 1-inch chunks. Alternately thread bell pepper, pineapple and chicken onto skewers. Place in shallow baking dish.

3. Combine chutney, orange juice, vanilla and nutmeg in small bowl; mix well. Pour over kabobs; cover. Refrigerate up to 4 hours.

4. Preheat broiler. Spray broiler pan with nonstick cooking spray; place kabobs on prepared broiler pan. Broil, 6 to 8 inches from heat, 4 to 5 minutes on each side or until chicken is no longer pink in center. Transfer to serving plates.

Makes 10 servings

Chicken Mango

4 boneless, skinless chicken breast halves
¾ teaspoon salt, divided
1 tablespoon lemon juice
¼ teaspoon pepper
2 eggs, well beaten
1½ cups fine dry bread crumbs
¼ cup CRISCO® Oil*
1 large ripe mango, peeled and pitted
⅓ cup honey
Juice of 1 large lemon
3 tablespoons soy sauce
2 cloves garlic

**Use your favorite Crisco Oil product.*

1. Rinse chicken; pat dry. Sprinkle with ¼ teaspoon salt. Place in bowl. Combine 1 tablespoon lemon juice, remaining ½ teaspoon salt and pepper. Pour over chicken. Toss to coat. Dip chicken in eggs, then crumbs.

2. Heat oil in large nonstick skillet on medium-high heat. Add chicken. Fry about 5 minutes per side or until golden brown and no longer pink in center. Drain on paper towels.

3. Place mango, honey, juice of 1 lemon, soy sauce and garlic in food processor. Process until blended, but not runny. Pour sauce into skillet. Bring to a boil on high heat. Reduce heat to low. Simmer 1 minute.

4. Cut chicken into strips. Dip in sauce.

Makes 4 servings

Caribbean Chutney Kabobs

Chunky Hawaiian Spread

1 package (3 ounces) light cream cheese, softened
½ cup fat free or light sour cream
1 can (8 ounces) DOLE® Crushed Pineapple, well-drained
¼ cup mango chutney*
Low fat crackers

**If there are large pieces of fruit in chutney, cut into small pieces.*

• Beat cream cheese, sour cream, crushed pineapple and chutney in bowl until blended. Cover and chill 1 hour or overnight. Serve with crackers. Refrigerate any leftover spread in airtight container for up to one week. *Makes 2½ cups*

Hot 'n' Chilly Mango Melon Soup

1 medium cantaloupe, seeded and cut into 2-inch pieces (4 cups)
2 mangos, seeded and cut into 2-inch pieces (2 cups)
1 cup plain yogurt
¼ cup honey
2 to 3 tablespoons *Frank's® RedHot®* Cayenne Pepper Sauce
1 tablespoon grated peeled fresh ginger
1 can (12 ounces) cold ginger ale

1. Combine cantaloupe and mango in blender or food processor. Cover; process until very smooth. (Process in batches if necessary.) Transfer to large bowl. Stir in yogurt, honey, ***Frank's RedHot*** Sauce and ginger. Cover; refrigerate at least 3 hours or overnight.

2. Stir in ginger ale just before serving. Garnish with mint, if desired. *Makes 6 cups*

Prep Time: 15 minutes
Chill Time: 3 hours

Chunky Hawaiian Spread

Coconut Chicken Tenders with Spicy Mango Salsa

- 1 firm ripe mango, peeled, seeded and chopped
- ½ cup chopped red bell pepper
- 3 tablespoons chopped green onion
- 2 tablespoons chopped fresh cilantro
- 1½ cups flaked coconut
- 1 egg
- 1 tablespoon vegetable oil
- ¼ teaspoon salt
- Dash ground red pepper
- ¾ pound chicken tenders

Combine mango, bell pepper, onion and cilantro in small bowl.

Season to taste with salt and ground red pepper. Transfer half of salsa to food processor; process until finely chopped (almost puréed). Combine with remaining salsa.

Preheat oven to 400°F. Spread coconut on large baking sheet. Bake 5 to 6 minutes or until lightly browned, stirring every 2 minutes. Transfer coconut to food processor; process until finely chopped but not pasty.

Beat egg with oil, salt and ground red pepper in small bowl. Add chicken tenders; toss to coat. Roll tenders in coconut; arrange on foil-lined baking sheet. Bake 18 to 20 minutes or until no longer pink in center. Serve with Spicy Mango Salsa.

Makes 5 to 6 servings

Wild Hawaiian Cocktail Meatballs

- 1 can (15¼ ounces) pineapple chunks in juice, undrained
- 14 ounces ground chicken
- 1 cup cooked wild rice
- ¼ cup finely chopped green bell pepper
- ¼ cup fine cracker crumbs
- 1 egg
- 1 teaspoon onion salt
- ¼ teaspoon ground ginger
- 1 tablespoon vegetable oil
- 1 cup sweet and sour sauce

Drain pineapple, reserving juice. In large bowl, combine chicken, wild rice, bell pepper, cracker crumbs, 2 tablespoons pineapple juice, egg, onion salt and ginger; mix well. Form mixture into 1-inch meatballs. In large skillet, heat oil over medium heat. Brown meatballs; drain. Add reserved pineapple and remaining juice; cover and cook over medium heat 10 to 15 minutes or until meatballs are no longer pink in center. Stir sweet and sour sauce into meatballs and pineapple; cook 4 to 5 minutes or until mixture is heated through. Serve with frilled toothpicks.

Makes 35 to 40 appetizers

Favorite recipe from **Minnesota Cultivated Wild Rice Council**

Coconut Chicken Tenders with Spicy Mango Salsa

Honeyed Pork and Mango Kabobs

½ cup honey
¼ cup frozen apple juice concentrate, thawed
3 tablespoons *Frank's® RedHot®* Cayenne Pepper Sauce
¼ teaspoon ground allspice
1 teaspoon grated lemon peel
1 pound pork tenderloin, cut into 1-inch cubes
1 large (12 ounces) ripe mango, peeled, pitted and cut into ¾-inch cubes, divided
½ cup frozen large baby onions, partially thawed

1. Combine honey, juice concentrate, ***Frank's RedHot*** Sauce and allspice in small saucepan. Bring to a boil over medium heat. Reduce heat to low; cook, stirring, 5 minutes. Stir in lemon peel. Remove from heat. Pour ¼ cup marinade into small bowl; reserve.

2. Place pork in large resealable plastic food storage bag. Pour remaining marinade over pork. Seal bag; refrigerate 1 hour. Prepare grill.

3. To prepare dipping sauce, place ¼ cup mango cubes in blender or food processor. Add reserved ¼ cup marinade. Cover; process until puréed. Transfer to serving bowl; set aside.

4. Alternately thread pork, remaining mango cubes and onions onto metal skewers. Place skewers on oiled grid. Grill,* over medium-low coals, 12 to 15 minutes or until pork is no longer pink. Serve kabobs with dipping sauce.

Makes 6 servings (¾ cup sauce)

**Or, broil 6 inches from heat 10 to 12 minutes or until pork is no longer pink.*

Note: You may substitute 1½ cups fresh or frozen peach cubes (2 to 3 peaches) for fresh mango.

Prep Time: 30 minutes
Marinate Time: 1 hour
Cook Time: about 20 minutes

Honey is one of the only foods that will never go bad, no mater how long you keep it. Be sure to store it in a tightly closed jar in a cool, dry place.

Honeyed Pork and Mango Kabobs

Coconut Fish Bites

1 cup flaked coconut
½ cup unsalted peanuts
1 egg
1 tablespoon soy sauce
¼ teaspoon salt
⅓ cup cornstarch
1 pound firm white fish (orange roughy, haddock or cod fish), cut into 1-inch cubes
Dipping Sauce (recipe follows)
1 quart vegetable oil for deep frying
Lemon wedges and fresh celery leaves for garnish

1. Place coconut and peanuts in food processor. Process using on/off pulsing action until peanuts are ground, but not pasty.

2. Blend egg, soy sauce and salt in pie plate. Place cornstarch and coconut mixture on separate pieces of waxed paper.

3. Toss fish cubes in cornstarch until well coated. Add to egg mixture; toss until coated with egg mixture. Lightly coat with coconut mixture. Refrigerate until ready to cook. Prepare Dipping Sauce.

4. Heat oil in heavy 3-quart saucepan over medium heat until deep-fat thermometer registers 365°F. Fry fish, in batches, 4 to 5 minutes or until golden brown and fish cubes flake easily when tested with fork. Adjust heat to maintain temperature. (Allow oil to return to 365°F between batches.) Drain on paper towels. Serve with Dipping Sauce. Garnish, if desired.

Makes about 24 appetizers

Dipping Sauce

1 can (8 ounces) sliced peaches, undrained
2 tablespoons packed brown sugar
2 tablespoons ketchup
1 tablespoon vinegar
1 tablespoon soy sauce
2 teaspoons cornstarch

Combine all ingredients in food processor. Process until peaches are chopped. Bring mixture to a boil in medium saucepan over medium heat; boil 1 minute or until thickened, stirring constantly. Sauce can be served warm or cold.

Makes about 1¼ cups

Coconut Fish Bites

Hawaiian Ribs

1 can (8 ounces) crushed pineapple in juice, undrained
⅓ cup apricot jam
3 tablespoons *French's®* Classic Yellow® Mustard
1 tablespoon red wine vinegar
2 teaspoons grated peeled fresh ginger
1 clove garlic, minced
3 to 4 pounds pork baby back ribs*

**Or, if baby back ribs are not available, substitute 4 pounds pork spareribs, cut in half lengthwise. Cut spareribs into 3- to 4-rib portions. Cook 20 minutes in enough boiling water to cover. Grill ribs 30 to 40 minutes or until no longer pink near bone, brushing with portion of pineapple mixture during last 10 minutes.*

1. Combine crushed pineapple with juice, apricot jam, mustard, vinegar, ginger and garlic in blender or food processor. Cover and process until very smooth.

2. Place ribs on oiled grid. Grill ribs over medium heat 40 minutes or until ribs are no longer pink near bone. Brush ribs with portion of pineapple sauce mixture during last 10 minutes of cooking. Cut into individual ribs to serve. Serve remaining sauce for dipping.

Makes 8 servings (1½ cups sauce)

Note: Try mixing 2 tablespoons ***French's®*** Mustard, any flavor, with ¾ cup peach-apricot sweet 'n' sour sauce to create a delicious luau fruit dip. Serve with assorted cut-up fresh fruit.

Prep Time: 10 minutes
Cook Time: 40 minutes

Island Mango Salsa

1 can (14.5 ounces) HUNT'S® Diced Tomatoes in Juice
2 medium ripe mangos, peeled and finely chopped
½ cup finely minced fresh cilantro
2 tablespoons grated onion
2 tablespoons lime juice
2 tablespoons tequila
2 teaspoons minced garlic
½ teaspoon cumin
½ teaspoon salt
½ teaspoon pepper
Baked tortilla chips

In a medium bowl, combine *all* ingredients. Cover and refrigerate at least 1 hour before serving. Stir once before serving. Serve with chips. *Makes 16 (¼ cup) servings*

Hawaiian Ribs

Grilled Spiced Halibut, Pineapple and Pepper Skewers

- **2 tablespoons lemon juice or lime juice**
- **1 teaspoon chili powder**
- **1 teaspoon minced garlic**
- **½ teaspoon ground cumin**
- **¼ teaspoon ground cinnamon**
- **⅛ teaspoon ground cloves**
- **½ pound boneless skinless halibut steak, about 1 inch thick**
- **½ small pineapple, peeled, halved lengthwise and cut into 24 pieces**
- **1 large green or red bell pepper, cut into 24 squares**

1. Combine lemon juice, chili powder, garlic, cumin, cinnamon and cloves in large resealable plastic food storage bag; knead until blended.

2. Rinse fish and pat dry. Cut into 12 cubes about 1 to 1¼ inches square. Add fish to bag; press out air and seal. Turn bag gently to coat fish with marinade. Refrigerate halibut 30 minutes to 1 hour. Soak 12 (6- to 8-inch) bamboo skewers in water while fish marinates.

3. Alternately thread 2 pieces pineapple, 2 pieces pepper and 1 piece fish onto each skewer.

4. Spray cold grid with nonstick cooking spray. Adjust grid 4 to 6 inches above heat. Preheat grill to medium-high heat. Place skewers on grill, cover if possible (or tent with foil) and grill 3 to 4 minutes or until grill marks appear on bottoms. Turn and grill skewers 3 to 4 minutes or until fish is opaque and flakes easily when tested with fork.

Makes 6 (2 skewers) servings

It is important to know what to look for when purchasing fresh fish. One can find fresh fish at most large supermarkets or at a retail fish market. An independent retail fish market usually buys its fish on a daily basis, whereas chain stores order in large quantities and often do not receive daily shipments.

Grilled Spiced Halibut, Pineapple and Pepper Skewers

Pineapple Ginger Shrimp Cocktail

9 fresh pineapple spears (about 1 package), divided
¼ cup all-fruit apricot preserves
1 tablespoon finely chopped onion
½ teaspoon grated fresh ginger
⅛ teaspoon black pepper
8 ounces cooked medium shrimp (about 30)
1 red or green bell pepper, cored and cut into 12 strips

1. Chop 3 pineapple spears into bite-sized pieces; combine with preserves, onion, ginger and black pepper in medium bowl.

2. Evenly arrange shrimp, bell pepper strips and remaining pineapple spears in 6 cocktail glasses. Evenly add pineapple mixture to each glass.

Makes 6 servings

Grapefruit and Shrimp with Zippy Cocktail Sauce

½ cup chili sauce
½ cup ketchup
1 to 2 teaspoons fresh grated SUNKIST® grapefruit peel
2 tablespoons fresh squeezed SUNKIST® grapefruit juice
2 to 3 SUNKIST® grapefruit, peeled, sectioned and chilled
1 pound medium to large shrimp, shelled, deveined, cooked and chilled

To prepare sauce, combine chili sauce, ketchup, grapefruit peel and grapefruit juice in small bowl; cover and chill. Arrange chilled grapefruit sections and shrimp in serving bowl. Serve sauce as dip for grapefruit sections and shrimp.

Makes about 1 cup sauce

Variation: Substitute fresh grated peel of 1 lemon and juice of ½ lemon for grapefruit peel and juice.

Pineapple Ginger Shrimp Cocktail

Jamaican Meat Patties

- **1 pound ground beef**
- **1 onion, chopped**
- **1 clove garlic, minced**
- **¼ cup *Frank's® RedHot®* Cayenne Pepper Sauce**
- **2¼ teaspoons curry powder, divided**
- **1 teaspoon dried thyme leaves**
- **1 egg, beaten**
- **2 sheets folded refrigerated unbaked pie crusts (15 ounce package)**

1. Cook beef, onion and garlic in nonstick skillet 5 minutes or until meat is browned, stirring to separate meat. Drain fat. Stir in ***Frank's RedHot*** Sauce, *½ cup water, 2 teaspoons* curry powder and thyme. Cook 5 minutes or until liquid is evaporated, stirring often. Cool slightly. Mix egg with *1 tablespoon water* and remaining *¼ teaspoon* curry powder; set aside.

2. Preheat oven to 400°F. Roll out each pie crust sheet into slightly larger round on lightly floured board. Cut out 10 rounds using 5-inch cookie cutter, re-rolling scraps as necessary. Brush edge of rounds with some of egg mixture. Spoon about 3 tablespoons cooled meat mixture in center of each round. Fold rounds in half, pressing edges with floured fork to seal.

3. Place patties onto lightly greased baking sheets. Brush tops with remaining egg mixture. Bake 15 minutes or until crusts are crisp. *Makes 10 patties*

Tip: A small bowl measuring 5-inches across may be used for the cookie cutter. Patties can be prepared ahead and frozen before baking; wrap securely. Bake, uncovered, at 400°F for 15 minutes. To make party-size appetizers, use a 3-inch round cutter.

Prep Time: 15 minutes
Cook Time: 25 minutes

Curry powder is formed by blending together a number of spices, including turmeric, cardamom, cumin, pepper, cloves, cinnamon, nutmeg and sometimes ginger. Chilies give it heat and ground dried garlic provides a depth of taste.

Luau Spareribs

6 pounds pork spareribs, cut into 3-rib portions

Pineapple Glaze & Dipping Sauce

1 can (20 ounces) crushed pineapple in juice, undrained

¾ cup apricot jam

¼ cup *Frank's® RedHot®* Cayenne Pepper Sauce

1 tablespoon grated peeled fresh ginger

1. Place spareribs in large pot. Add enough water to cover. Bring to a boil; reduce heat. Simmer, covered, 20 minutes or until ribs are tender; drain.

2. Prepare Pineapple Glaze & Dipping Sauce. Combine pineapple with juice, jam, ***Frank's RedHot*** Sauce and ginger in blender or food processor. Cover; process until puréed. Pour *1½ cups* sauce into serving bowl; reserve for dipping.

3. Preheat oven to 350°F. Arrange ribs in shallow roasting pan. Brush both sides of ribs with some of the remaining sauce. Bake, uncovered, 20 minutes or until ribs are glazed and heated through, basting often. Serve ribs with reserved dipping sauce.

Makes 6 servings

Ribs may be finished on the grill or in the broiler. Cook over medium heat, basting often with sauce.

Prep Time: 15 minutes
Cook Time: 1 hour 30 minutes

Pineapple-Mango Salsa

1½ cups DOLE® Fresh Pineapple Chunks

1 ripe DOLE® Mango, peeled and chopped

½ cup chopped red cabbage

⅓ cup finely chopped DOLE® Red Onion

¼ cup chopped fresh cilantro

2 tablespoons lime juice

1 to 2 serrano or jalapeño chiles, seeded and minced

• Stir together pineapple chunks, mango, cabbage, red onion, cilantro, lime juice and chiles in medium bowl. Cover and chill for at least 30 minutes to blend flavors. Serve salsa over grilled chicken with grilled vegetables. Garnish with lime wedges, if desired.

• Salsa can also be served as a dip with tortilla chips or spooned over quesadillas or tacos.

Makes 3½ cups

Prep Time: 15 minutes
Chill Time: 30 minutes

That's Italian

Mediterranean Frittata

¼ cup olive oil
5 small yellow onions, thinly sliced
1 can (14½ ounces) whole peeled tomatoes, drained and chopped
¼ pound prosciutto or cooked ham, chopped
¼ cup grated Parmesan cheese
2 tablespoons chopped fresh parsley
½ teaspoon dried marjoram leaves
¼ teaspoon dried basil leaves
¼ teaspoon salt
Generous dash black pepper
6 eggs
2 tablespoons butter or margarine
Italian parsley leaves for garnish

1. Heat oil in medium skillet over medium-high heat. Cook and stir onions in hot oil 6 to 8 minutes until soft and golden. Add tomatoes. Cook and stir over medium heat 5 minutes. Remove tomatoes and onions to large bowl with slotted spoon; discard drippings. Cool tomato-onion mixture to room temperature.

2. Stir prosciutto, cheese, parsley, marjoram, basil, salt and pepper into cooled tomato-onion mixture. Whisk eggs in small bowl; stir into prosciutto mixture.

3. Preheat broiler. Heat butter in large broilerproof skillet over medium heat until melted and bubbly; reduce heat to low.

4. Add egg mixture to skillet, spreading evenly. Cook over low heat 8 to 10 minutes until all but top ¼ inch of egg mixture is set; shake pan gently to test. *Do not stir.*

5. Broil egg mixture about 4 inches from heat 1 to 2 minutes until top of egg mixture is set. (Do not brown or frittata will be dry.) Frittata can be served hot, at room temperature or cold. To serve, cut into wedges. Garnish, if desired.

Makes 6 to 8 appetizer servings

Mediterranean Frittata

Tortellini Teasers

Zesty Tomato Sauce (recipe follows)
½ (9-ounce) package refrigerated cheese tortellini
1 large red or green bell pepper, cut into 1-inch pieces
2 medium carrots, peeled and sliced ½ inch thick
1 medium zucchini, sliced ½ inch thick
12 medium fresh mushrooms
12 cherry tomatoes

1. Prepare Zesty Tomato Sauce; keep warm.

2. Cook tortellini according to package directions; drain.

3. Alternate 1 tortellini and 2 to 3 vegetable pieces on long frilled wooden picks or wooden skewers. Serve as dippers with tomato sauce.

Makes 6 servings

Zesty Tomato Sauce

1 can (15 ounces) tomato purée
2 tablespoons finely chopped onion
2 tablespoons chopped fresh parsley
1 teaspoon dried oregano leaves
¼ teaspoon dried thyme leaves
¼ teaspoon salt
⅛ teaspoon black pepper

Combine tomato purée, onion, parsley, oregano and thyme in small saucepan. Heat thoroughly, stirring occasionally. Stir in salt and pepper. Garnish with carrot curl, if desired.

Noodles originated in Germany in the 13th century. Noodles derive their name from the German word *Nudel* that means a pasta product made with eggs and shaped in ribbons.

Tortellini Teasers

Fried Calamari with Tartar Sauce

1 pound fresh or thawed frozen squid
1 egg
1 tablespoon milk
¾ cup fine dry unseasoned bread crumbs
Vegetable oil
Tartar Sauce (recipe page 70)
Lemon wedges (optional)

1. To clean each squid, hold body of squid firmly in one hand. Grasp head firmly with other hand; pull head, twisting gently from side to side. (Head and contents of body should pull away in one piece.) Set aside tubular body sac. Cut tentacles off head; set aside. Discard head and contents of body.

2. Grasp tip of pointed, thin, clear cartilage protruding from body; pull out and discard. Rinse squid under cold running water. Peel off and discard spotted outer membrane covering body sac and fins. Pull off side fins; set aside. Rinse inside of squid body thoroughly under running water. Repeat with remaining squid.

3. Cut each squid body crosswise into ¼-inch rings. Cut reserved fins into thin slices. (Body rings, fins and reserved tentacles are all edible parts.) Pat pieces thoroughly dry with paper towels.

4. Beat egg with milk in small bowl. Add squid pieces; stir to coat well. Spread bread crumbs on plate. Dip squid pieces in bread crumbs; place in shallow bowl or on waxed paper. Let stand 10 to 15 minutes before frying.

5. To deep fry squid,* heat 1½ inches oil in large saucepan to 350°F. (Caution: Squid will pop and spatter during frying; do not stand too close to pan.) Adjust heat to maintain temperature. Fry 8 to 10 pieces of squid at a time in hot oil 45 to 60 seconds until light brown. Remove with slotted spoon; drain on paper towels. Repeat with remaining squid pieces.

6. Serve hot with Tartar Sauce and lemon wedges. Garnish as desired.

Makes 2 to 3 servings

**To shallow fry squid, heat about ¼ inch oil in large skillet over medium-high heat; reduce heat to medium. Add as many pieces of squid in single layer without crowding to hot oil. Cook, turning once with 2 forks, 1 minute per side or until light brown. Proceed as directed in step 5. (This method uses less oil but requires slightly more hand work.)*

continued on page 70

Fried Calamari with Tartar Sauce

Fried Calamari with Tartar Sauce, continued

Tartar Sauce

1 green onion
1 tablespoon drained capers
1 small sweet gherkin or pickle
2 tablespoons chopped fresh parsley
1⅓ cups mayonnaise

1. Thinly slice green onion. Mince capers and gherkin.

2. Fold green onion, capers, gherkin and parsley into mayonnaise. Cover and refrigerate until ready to serve.

Makes about 1⅓ cups

Zesty Pesto Cheese Spread

2 packages (8 ounces each) cream cheese, softened
1 cup shredded mozzarella cheese
1 cup chopped fresh basil or parsley
½ cup grated Parmesan cheese
½ cup toasted pine nuts*
⅓ cup *French's*® Napa Valley Style Dijon Mustard
1 clove garlic

**To toast pine nuts, place nuts on baking sheet. Bake at 350°F 8 to 10 minutes or until lightly golden or microwave on microwavable dish on HIGH (100%) 1 minute.*

1. Combine cream cheese, mozzarella, basil, Parmesan, pine nuts, mustard and garlic in food processor. Cover and process until smooth and well blended.

2. Spoon pesto spread into serving bowl or crock. Spread on crackers or serve with vegetable crudites.

Makes 3¼ cups spread

Serving Variations: Pesto spread may also be piped into cherry tomatoes using pastry bag fitted with decorative tip. Or, use as filling in rolled flour tortillas.

Prep Time: 15 minutes

Bruschetta with Summer Flavors

4 cloves Grilled Garlic (recipe follows), mashed
4 plum tomatoes, cut lengthwise into halves
1 small red, yellow or orange bell pepper
½ cup chopped fresh basil
Olive oil
2 teaspoons lemon juice
Salt and black pepper
4 thick slices country-style Italian bread
4 teaspoons kalamata olive spread*

**Kalamata olive spread can be purchased in jars or prepared at home. To prepare, place 1 drained 6-ounce jar of pitted kalamata olives (about 1½ cups), 2 tablespoons olive oil, 2 tablespoons drained capers, 1 large clove garlic and ½ teaspoon dried oregano leaves in food processor; blend until smooth. Refrigerate in covered container up to 1 month. Makes about 1 cup.*

Prepared Grilled Garlic. Place tomatoes and bell pepper over medium-hot KINGSFORD® Briquets on covered grill. Grill tomatoes 2 to 3 minutes per side, removing while warm but still firm. Grill bell pepper 15 to 20 minutes until charred on all sides. Place in large resealable plastic food storage bag; seal. Let stand 15 minutes; remove skin. Remove and discard seeds; cut pepper into ¼-inch strips. Coarsely chop grilled tomatoes and place in small bowl; add garlic, basil, 2 tablespoons oil, lemon juice, and salt and black pepper to taste. Brush bread lightly with additional olive oil. Grill bread over medium Kingsford briquets until toasted, turning once. Spread each slice with 1 teaspoon kalamata olive spread. Top with tomato mixture and bell pepper, dividing equally. *Makes 4 servings*

Note: Vegetables can be grilled in advance and refrigerated until ready to use.

Grilled Garlic

1 or 2 heads garlic
Olive oil

Peel outermost papery skin from garlic heads. Brush heads with oil. Grill heads at edge of grid on covered grill over medium-hot KINGSFORD® Briquets 30 to 45 minutes or until cloves are soft and buttery. Remove from grill; cool slightly. Gently squeeze softened garlic head from root end so that cloves slip out of skins into small bowl. Use immediately or cover and refrigerate up to 1 week.

Crostini

¼ loaf whole wheat baguette (4 ounces)
4 plum tomatoes
1 cup (4 ounces) shredded part-skim mozzarella cheese
3 tablespoons prepared pesto sauce

1. Preheat oven to 400°F. Slice baguette into 16 very thin, diagonal slices. Slice each tomato vertically into four ¼-inch slices.

2. Place baguette slices on nonstick baking sheet. Top each with 1 tablespoon cheese, then 1 slice tomato. Bake about 8 minutes or until bread is lightly toasted and cheese is melted. Remove from oven; top each crostini with about ½ teaspoon pesto sauce. Garnish with fresh basil, if desired. Serve warm.

Makes 8 appetizer servings

Fresh Tomato Pasta Andrew

1 pound fresh tomatoes, cut into wedges
1 cup packed fresh basil leaves
2 cloves garlic, chopped
2 tablespoons olive oil
8 ounces Camenzola cheese *or* 6 ounces ripe Brie cheese, cut into small pieces
2 ounces Stilton cheese, cut into small pieces
Salt and white pepper to taste
4 ounces uncooked angel hair pasta, vermicelli or other thin pasta
Freshly grated Parmesan cheese
Additional fresh basil leaves for garnish

1. Place tomatoes, 1 cup basil, garlic and oil in food processor or blender; process until ingredients are roughly chopped, but not puréed.

2. Combine tomato mixture with Camenzola cheese and Stilton cheese in large bowl; season with salt and pepper.

3. Cook pasta according to package directions until tender but still firm; rinse and drain.

4. Top hot pasta with tomato-cheese mixture and serve with Parmesan cheese. Garnish, if desired.

Makes 4 first-course servings

Crostini

Grilled Baby Artichokes with Pepper Dip

18 baby artichokes* (about 1½ pounds)
½ teaspoon salt
¼ cup *Frank's® RedHot®* Cayenne Pepper Sauce
¼ cup butter or margarine, melted
Roasted Pepper Dip (recipe follows)

**You may substitute 2 packages (9 ounces each) frozen artichoke halves, thawed and drained. Do not microwave. Brush with Frank's® RedHot® butter mixture and grill as directed below.*

1. Wash and trim tough outer leaves from artichokes. Cut ½-inch off top of artichokes, then cut in half lengthwise. Place artichoke halves, 1 cup water and salt in 3-quart microwavable bowl. Cover; microwave on HIGH 8 minutes or until just tender. Thread artichoke halves onto metal skewers.

2. Prepare grill. Combine ***Frank's RedHot*** Sauce and butter in small bowl. Brush mixture over artichokes. Place artichokes on grid. Grill, over hot coals, 5 minutes or until tender, turning and basting often with sauce mixture. Serve artichokes with Roasted Pepper Dip.

Makes 6 servings

Prep Time: 20 minutes
Cook Time: 13 minutes

Roasted Pepper Dip

1 jar (7 ounces) roasted red peppers, drained
1 clove garlic, chopped
¼ cup reduced-fat mayonnaise
2 tablespoons *French's®* Napa Valley Style Dijon Mustard
2 tablespoons *Frank's® RedHot®* Cayenne Pepper Sauce
¼ teaspoon salt

1. Place roasted peppers and garlic in food processor or blender. Cover; process on high until very smooth.

2. Add mayonnaise, mustard, ***Frank's RedHot*** Sauce and salt. Process until well blended. Cover; refrigerate 30 minutes.

Makes about 1 cup

Prep Time: 10 minutes
Chill Time: 30 minutes

Grilled Baby Artichokes with Pepper Dip

Pizza Breadsticks

- **1 package (¼ ounce) active dry yeast**
- **¾ cup warm water (105° to 115°F)**
- **2½ cups all-purpose flour**
- **½ cup (2 ounces) shredded part-skim mozzarella cheese**
- **¼ cup (1 ounce) shredded Parmesan cheese**
- **¼ cup chopped red bell pepper**
- **1 green onion with top, sliced**
- **1 medium clove garlic, minced**
- **½ teaspoon dried basil leaves, crushed**
- **½ teaspoon dried oregano leaves, crushed**
- **¼ teaspoon salt**
- **¼ teaspoon red pepper flakes (optional)**
- **1 tablespoon olive oil**

1. Preheat oven to 400°F. Spray 2 large nonstick baking sheets with nonstick cooking spray; set aside.

2. Sprinkle yeast over warm water in small bowl; stir until yeast dissolves. Let stand 5 minutes or until bubbly.

3. Meanwhile, place all remaining ingredients except olive oil in food processor; process a few seconds to combine. With food processor running, gradually add yeast mixture and olive oil. Process just until mixture forms a ball. (Add an additional 2 tablespoons flour if dough is too sticky.)

4. Transfer dough to lightly floured surface; knead 1 minute. Let dough rest 5 minutes. Roll out dough with lightly floured rolling pin to form 14×8-inch rectangle; cut dough crosswise into ½-inch-wide strips. Twist dough strips; place on prepared baking sheets.

5. Bake 14 to 16 minutes or until lightly browned.

Makes 14 servings

Carpaccio di Zucchini

- **¾ pound zucchini, shredded**
- **½ cup sliced almonds, toasted**
- **1 tablespoon prepared Italian dressing**
- **4 French bread baguettes, sliced in half lengthwise**
- **4 teaspoons soft spread margarine**
- **3 tablespoons grated Parmesan cheese**

1. Preheat broiler. Place zucchini in medium bowl. Add almonds and dressing; mix well. Set aside.

2. Place baguette halves on large baking sheet; spread evenly with margarine. Sprinkle with cheese. Broil 3 inches from heat 2 to 3 minutes or until edges and cheese are browned.

3. Spread zucchini mixture evenly on each baguette half. Serve immediately.

Makes 4 servings

Go-with suggestions: Spaghetti with tomato sauce.

Prep and Cook Time: 28 minutes

Pizza Breadsticks

Bruschetta

Nonstick cooking spray
1 cup thinly sliced onion
½ cup chopped seeded tomato
2 tablespoons capers
¼ teaspoon black pepper
3 cloves garlic, finely chopped
1 teaspoon olive oil
4 slices French bread
½ cup (2 ounces) shredded reduced-fat Monterey Jack cheese

1. Spray large nonstick skillet with cooking spray. Heat over medium heat until hot. Add onion. Cook and stir 5 minutes. Stir in tomato, capers and pepper. Cook 3 minutes.

2. Preheat broiler. Combine garlic and oil in small bowl; brush bread slices with mixture. Top with onion mixture; sprinkle with cheese. Place on baking sheet. Broil 3 minutes or until cheese melts. *Makes 4 servings*

Fra Diavolo Antipasto Salad

1 cup prepared Italian salad dressing
3 to 4 tablespoons *Frank's® RedHot®* Cayenne Pepper Sauce or to taste
¼ cup chopped fresh Italian parsley
6 cups assorted vegetables, such as cauliflower, carrots, tomatoes, celery, zucchini and/or mushrooms, cut into bite-size pieces
1 jar (6 ounces) Tuscan peppers, drained
¼ pound mild provolone cheese, cut into small sticks
¼ pound fresh mozzarella cheese, cut into small cubes*
¼ pound hard salami, cut into small cubes
Romaine lettuce leaves

**Look for fresh mozzarella in the deli section of your supermarket.*

Whisk together salad dressing, ***Frank's RedHot*** Sauce and parsley in small bowl. Place vegetables, peppers, cheeses and salami in large bowl. Add dressing; toss well to coat evenly. Cover and marinate in refrigerator 1 hour. Arrange lettuce on large platter. Spoon salad over lettuce just before serving.
Makes 6 appetizer servings

Prep Time: 20 minutes
Marinate Time: 1 hour

Bruschetta

Venetian Canapés

- **12 slices firm white bread**
- **5 tablespoons butter or margarine, divided**
- **2 tablespoons all-purpose flour**
- **½ cup milk**
- **3 ounces fresh mushrooms (about 9 medium), finely chopped**
- **6 tablespoons grated Parmesan cheese, divided**
- **2 teaspoons anchovy paste**
- **¼ teaspoon salt**
- **⅛ teaspoon black pepper**
- **Green and ripe olive slices, red and green bell pepper strips and rolled anchovy fillets, for garnish**

Preheat oven to 350°F. Cut 2 rounds out of each bread slice with 2-inch round cutter. Melt 3 tablespoons butter in small saucepan. Brush both sides of bread rounds lightly with butter. Bake bread rounds on ungreased baking sheet 5 to 6 minutes per side or until golden. Remove to wire rack. Cool completely. *Increase oven temperature to 425°F.*

Melt remaining 2 tablespoons butter in same small saucepan. Stir in flour; cook and stir over medium heat until bubbly. Whisk in milk; cook and stir 1 minute or until sauce thickens and bubbles. (Sauce will be very thick.) Place mushrooms in large bowl; stir in sauce, 3 tablespoons cheese, anchovy paste, salt and black pepper until well blended.

Spread 1 heaping teaspoon mushroom mixture onto each toast round; place on ungreased baking sheets. Sprinkle remaining 3 tablespoons cheese over bread rounds, dividing evenly. Bake 5 to 7 minutes or until tops are light brown. Serve warm.

Makes 8 to 10 appetizer servings (about 2 dozen)

Fast Pesto Focaccia

- **1 can (10 ounces) pizza crust dough**
- **2 tablespoons prepared pesto**
- **4 sun-dried tomatoes packed in oil, drained**

1. Preheat oven to 425°F. Lightly grease 8×8×2-inch pan. Unroll pizza dough; fold in half and pat into pan.

2. Spread pesto evenly over dough. Chop tomatoes or snip with kitchen scissors; sprinkle over pesto. Press tomatoes into dough. Make indentations in dough every 2 inches using wooden spoon handle.

3. Bake 10 to 12 minutes or until golden brown. Cut into squares and serve warm or at room temperature.

Makes 16 squares

Prep and Cook Time: 20 minutes

Venetian Canapés

Chicken Parmesan Stromboli

- **1 pound boneless, skinless chicken breast halves**
- **½ teaspoon salt**
- **¼ teaspoon ground black pepper**
- **2 teaspoons BERTOLLI® Olive Oil**
- **2 cups shredded mozzarella cheese (about 8 ounces)**
- **1 jar (1 pound 10 ounces) RAGÚ® Chunky Gardenstyle Pasta Sauce, divided**
- **2 tablespoons grated Parmesan cheese**
- **1 tablespoon finely chopped fresh parsley**
- **1 pound fresh or thawed frozen bread dough**

1. Preheat oven to 400°F. Season chicken with salt and pepper. In 12-inch skillet, heat oil over medium-high heat and brown chicken. Remove chicken from skillet and let cool; pull into large shreds.

2. In medium bowl, combine chicken, mozzarella cheese, ½ cup Ragú® Chunky Gardenstyle Pasta Sauce, Parmesan cheese and parsley; set aside.

3. On greased jelly-roll pan, press dough to form 12×10-inch rectangle. Arrange chicken mixture down center of dough. Cover filling bringing one long side into center, then overlap with the other long side; pinch seam to seal. Fold in ends and pinch to seal. Arrange on pan, seam-side down. Gently press in sides to form 12×4-inch loaf. Bake 35 minutes or until dough is cooked and golden. Cut stromboli into slices. Heat remaining pasta sauce and serve with stromboli. *Makes 6 servings*

Clams Diablo

- **2 tablespoons olive or vegetable oil**
- **½ cup chopped onion**
- **1 clove garlic, minced**
- **1 can (14.5 ounces) CONTADINA® Recipe Ready Diced Tomatoes, undrained**
- **¼ cup dry red wine or chicken broth**
- **½ teaspoon dried thyme leaves, crushed**
- **¼ teaspoon salt**
- **¼ teaspoon crushed red pepper flakes**
- **1½ pounds scrubbed fresh clams**
- **2 tablespoons chopped fresh parsley *or* 2 teaspoons dried parsley flakes**

1. Heat oil in medium skillet. Add onion and garlic; sauté for 1 minute.

2. Stir in undrained tomatoes, wine, thyme, salt and red pepper flakes. Bring to a boil.

3. Reduce heat to low; simmer, uncovered, for 10 minutes, stirring occasionally.

4. Add clams; cover. Simmer for 5 minutes or just until clams open. Sprinkle with parsley just before serving.

Makes about 4 to 6 servings

Prep Time: 8 minutes
Cook Time: 17 minutes

Chicken Parmesan Stromboli

Pizzette with Basil

1 can (6 ounces) CONTADINA® Italian Paste with Italian Seasonings
2 tablespoons softened cream cheese
2 tablespoons chopped fresh basil *or* 2 teaspoons dried basil leaves
1 loaf (1 pound) Italian bread, sliced ¼ inch thick
8 ounces mozzarella cheese, thinly sliced
Whole basil leaves (optional)
Freshly ground black pepper (optional)

1. Combine tomato paste, cream cheese and chopped basil in small bowl.

2. Toast bread slices on *ungreased* baking sheet under broiler, 6 to 8 inches from heat, turning after 1 minute, until lightly browned on both sides; remove from broiler.

3. Spread 2 teaspoons tomato mixture onto each toasted bread slice; top with 1 slice (about ¼ ounce) mozzarella cheese.

4. Broil 6 to 8 inches from heat for 1 to 2 minutes or until cheese begins to melt. Top with whole basil leaves and pepper, if desired. *Makes about 30 pizzettes*

Prep Time: 7 minutes
Cook Time: 10 minutes

Pesto Chicken Brushetta

2 tablespoons olive oil, divided
1 teaspoon coarsely chopped garlic, divided
8 diagonal slices (¼ inch thick) sourdough bread
½ cup (2 ounces) grated BELGIOIOSO® Asiago Cheese, divided
2 tablespoons prepared pesto
¼ teaspoon pepper
4 boneless skinless chicken breast halves
12 slices (¼ inch thick) BELGIOIOSO® Fresh Mozzarella Cheese (8 ounces)
2 tomatoes, each cut into 4 slices

In 10-inch skillet, heat 1 tablespoon olive oil and ½ teaspoon garlic. Add 4 slices bread. Cook over medium-high heat, turning once, 5 to 7 minutes or until toasted. Remove from pan. Add remaining 1 tablespoon oil and ½ teaspoon garlic; repeat with remaining bread slices. Sprinkle ¼ cup BelGioioso Asiago Cheese on bread. In same skillet, combine pesto and pepper. Add chicken, coating with pesto. Cook over medium-high heat, turning once, 8 to 10 minutes or until chicken is brown. Place 3 slices BelGioioso Fresh Mozzarella Cheese on each bread slice; top with tomato slice. Slice chicken pieces in half horizontally; place on tomato. Sprinkle with remaining BelGioioso Asiago Cheese. *Makes 4 servings*

Pizzettes with Basil

Parmesan Polenta

4 cups chicken broth
1 small onion, minced
4 cloves garlic, minced
1 tablespoon minced fresh rosemary *or* 1 teaspoon dried rosemary
½ teaspoon salt
1¼ cups yellow cornmeal
6 tablespoons grated Parmesan cheese
1 tablespoon olive oil, divided

1. Spray 11×7-inch baking pan with nonstick cooking spray; set aside. Spray one side of 7-inch-long sheet of waxed paper with cooking spray; set aside. Combine chicken broth, onion, garlic, rosemary and salt in medium saucepan. Bring to a boil over high heat; add cornmeal gradually, stirring constantly. Reduce heat to medium and simmer 30 minutes or until mixture has consistency of thick mashed potatoes. Remove from heat and stir in cheese.

2. Spread polenta evenly in prepared pan; place waxed paper, sprayed-side down, on polenta and smooth. (If surface is bumpy, it is more likely to stick to grill.) Cool on wire rack 15 minutes or until firm. Remove waxed paper; cut into 6 squares. Remove squares from pan.

3. To prevent sticking, spray grid with cooking spray. Prepare coals for grilling. Brush tops of squares with half the oil. Grill oil-side down on covered grill over medium to low coals for 6 to 8 minutes or until golden. Brush with remaining oil and gently turn over. Grill 6 to 8 minutes more or until golden. Serve warm.

Makes 6 servings

Polenta, an integral part of Northern Italian cuisine, is made from cornmeal and may be served as a hot cereal or side dish with butter and sometimes Parmesan cheese. When allowed to cool and become firm, it can be sliced or cut into squares and fried, broiled or baked. Fried polenta is usually eaten as a first course or a side dish often topped with tomato sauce or a mushroom or other vegetable mixture.

Parmesan Polenta

Sausage Pizza Piena

1 tablespoon olive oil
1 onion, chopped
1 red bell pepper, diced
1 green bell pepper, diced
1 pound turkey sausage, casing removed
1 teaspoon dried marjoram leaves
1 pound thawed frozen bread dough, at room temperature
2 cups (8 ounces) shredded mozzarella cheese
2 eggs, lightly beaten
3 tablespoons *Frank's® RedHot®* Cayenne Pepper Sauce
1 tablespoon milk
Grated Parmesan cheese
Sesame seeds

1. Heat oil in large nonstick skillet. Add onion and bell peppers; cook 5 minutes or until tender. Add sausage and marjoram. Cook and stir 5 minutes or until meat is no longer pink. Drain well; cool.

2. Preheat oven to 375°F. Cut dough in half. Roll half of dough into 14×10-inch rectangle on lightly floured board. (Let dough rest 5 minutes if dough springs back when rolling.) Pat onto bottom and 1-inch up sides of greased 13×9×2-inch baking pan. Roll out remaining half of dough to 13×9-inch rectangle; keep covered.

3. Stir cheese, eggs and ***Frank's RedHot*** Sauce into sausage mixture; toss to coat evenly. Spoon evenly over bottom dough. Cover sausage mixture with top half of dough. Pinch top and bottom edges of dough to seal. Brush top lightly with milk. Sprinkle with Parmesan cheese and sesame seeds.

4. Bake 25 minutes or until golden and bread sounds hollow when tapped. Let stand 10 minutes. Cut into squares to serve.

Makes 6 to 8 servings

Prep Time: 30 minutes
Bake Time: 25 minutes

Sausage Pizza Piena

Grilled Garlic & Herb Pizzas

- Homemade Pizza Dough (recipe page 92)
- 8 cloves Grilled Garlic (recipe page 92)
- 1 medium yellow onion
- Olive oil
- 1 medium red, yellow or orange bell pepper
- 1 cup crumbled goat cheese
- ¼ cup chopped fresh herb mixture (thyme, basil, oregano and parsley) *or* 4 teaspoons dry herb mixture
- ¼ cup grated Parmesan cheese

Prepare Homemade Pizza Dough. While dough is rising, light KINGSFORD® Briquets in covered grill. Arrange medium-hot briquets on one side of the grill. Prepare Grilled Garlic. Lightly oil grid to prevent sticking. Cut onion into ½-inch-thick slices. Insert wooden picks into onion slices from edges to prevent separating into rings. (Soak wooden picks in hot water 15 minutes to prevent burning.) Brush onion lightly with oil. Place whole bell pepper and onion slices on grid around edge of briquets. Grill, covered, 20 to 30 minutes until tender, turning once or twice. Remove picks from onion slices and separate into rings. Cut pepper in half and remove seeds when cool enough to handle; slice pepper halves into strips.

Roll or gently stretch each ball of dough into 7-inch round. Brush lightly with oil on both sides. Grill dough on grid directly above medium-hot KINGSFORD® Briquets 1 to 3 minutes or until dough starts to bubble and bottom is lightly browned. Turn; grill 3 to 5 minutes or until second side is lightly browned and dough is cooked through. Remove from grill. Spread 2 cloves Grilled Garlic onto each crust; top with onion rings, pepper strips, goat cheese, herbs and Parmesan cheese, dividing equally. Place pizzas around edge of coals; grill, covered, 5 minutes until bottom crust is crisp, cheese melts and toppings are heated through. *Makes 4 individual pizzas*

Note: A 1-pound loaf of frozen bread dough, thawed, can be substituted for Homemade Pizza Dough. Or, substitute 4 pre-baked individual Italian bread shells, add toppings and warm on the grill.

continued on page 92

Grilled Garlic & Herb Pizzas

Grilled Garlic

1 or 2 heads garlic
Olive oil

Peel outermost papery skin from garlic heads. Brush heads with oil. Grill heads at edge of grid on covered grill over medium-hot KINGSFORD® Briquets 30 to 45 minutes or until cloves are soft and buttery. Remove from grill; cool slightly. Gently squeeze softened garlic heads from root end so that cloves slip out of skins into small bowl. Use immediately or cover and refrigerate up to 1 week.

Homemade Pizza Dough

2¾ cups all-purpose flour, divided
1 package quick-rising yeast
¾ teaspoon salt
1 cup water
1½ tablespoons vegetable oil

Combine 1½ cups flour, yeast and salt in food processor. Heat water and oil in small saucepan until 120° to 130°F. With food processor running, add water and oil to flour mixture; process 30 seconds. Add 1 cup flour; process until dough comes together to form ball. Knead on floured board 3 to 4 minutes or until smooth and satiny, kneading in as much of the remaining ¼ cup flour as needed to prevent dough from sticking. Place dough in oiled bowl, turning once. Cover with towel; let rise in warm place 30 minutes until doubled in bulk. Divide dough into 4 equal balls.

Artichoke Hearts Marinara

1 pound baby artichokes (about 12)
1 lemon half
2 tablespoons olive oil
½ cup chopped onion
1 clove garlic, minced
½ cup chicken broth
1 cup prepared marinara or spaghetti sauce
¼ cup freshly grated Parmesan cheese
Lemon wedges and artichoke leaves for garnish

1. To prepare baby artichokes, rinse under running water. Bend back outer green leaves and snap off at base. Continue snapping off leaves until top halves of leaves are green and bottom halves are yellow.

2. Cut off green fibrous tops of leaves, parallel to base; discard tips. Cut stem off, level with base. Cut in half lengthwise (from top). To help prevent discoloration, rub ends with lemon.

3. Heat oil in large skillet over medium-high heat. Cook and stir artichoke hearts, onion and garlic in hot oil 5 to 10 minutes until onion is soft and golden. Add broth; cover. Bring to a boil over high heat; reduce heat to medium-low. Simmer 10 to 15 minutes. Uncover and boil until liquid has evaporated.

4. Preheat broiler. Spread marinara sauce in bottom of 8-inch square broilerproof baking dish or 4 individual broilerproof serving dishes. Arrange artichoke hearts cut side down in sauce. Sprinkle with cheese. Brown under broiler about 5 minutes or until sauce is heated through and cheese is melted. Garnish, if desired. Serve immediately.

Makes 4 appetizer or side-dish servings

To serve as a main course, prepare 1/2 pound fettuccine or spaghetti according to package directions. Divide pasta between two warm plates and pour 1/2 of artichoke hearts mixture over each serving.

Antipasto with Marinated Mushrooms

1 recipe Marinated Mushrooms (recipe follows)
4 teaspoons red wine vinegar
½ teaspoon dried basil leaves
½ teaspoon dried oregano leaves
Generous dash black pepper
¼ cup olive oil
4 ounces mozzarella cheese, cut into ½-inch cubes
4 ounces prosciutto or cooked ham, thinly sliced
4 ounces provolone cheese, cut into 2-inch sticks
1 jar (10 ounces) pepperoncini peppers, drained
8 ounces hard salami, thinly sliced
2 jars (6 ounces each) marinated artichoke hearts, drained
1 can (6 ounces) pitted ripe olives, drained
Fresh basil leaves and chives, for garnish

Prepare Marinated Mushrooms; set aside. Combine vinegar, dried basil, oregano and black pepper in small bowl. Whisk in oil until well blended. Add mozzarella cubes; stir to coat. Marinate, covered, in refrigerator at least 2 hours.

Drain mozzarella cubes; reserve marinade. Wrap ½ of prosciutto slices around provolone sticks; roll up remaining slices separately. Arrange mozzarella cubes, prosciutto-wrapped provolone sticks, prosciutto rolls, Marinated Mushrooms, pepperoncini, salami, artichoke hearts and olives on large platter lined with lettuce, if desired. Drizzle reserved marinade over pepperoncini, artichoke hearts and olives. Garnish, if desired. Serve with small forks or wooden toothpicks.

Makes 6 to 8 servings

Marinated Mushrooms

3 tablespoons lemon juice
2 tablespoons chopped fresh parsley
½ teaspoon salt
¼ teaspoon dried tarragon leaves
1 clove garlic, slightly crushed
⅛ teaspoon black pepper
½ cup olive oil
½ pound small or medium fresh mushrooms, stems removed

Combine lemon juice, parsley, salt, tarragon, garlic and pepper in medium bowl. Whisk in oil until well blended. Add mushrooms; stir to coat. Marinate, covered, in refrigerator 4 hours or overnight, stirring occasionally. Drain mushrooms; reserve marinade for dressing, if desired.

Antipasto with Marinated Mushrooms

Focaccia

$1\frac{1}{2}$ cups warm water (105 to 110°F)
1 package active dry yeast
1 teaspoon sugar
4 cups all-purpose flour, divided
7 tablespoons olive oil, divided
1 teaspoon salt
$\frac{1}{4}$ cup bottled roasted red peppers, drained and cut into strips
$\frac{1}{4}$ cup pitted black olives

To proof yeast, sprinkle yeast and sugar over warm water in large bowl; stir until dissolved. Let stand 5 minutes or until mixture is bubbly. Add $3\frac{1}{2}$ cups flour, 3 tablespoons oil and salt, stirring until soft dough forms. Turn out dough onto lightly floured surface. Knead 5 minutes or until smooth and elastic, gradually adding remaining flour to prevent sticking, if necessary. Shape dough into ball; place in large, lightly greased bowl. Turn dough over so top is greased. Cover with towel; let rise in warm place 1 hour or until doubled in bulk.

Brush $15\frac{1}{2}\times10\frac{1}{2}$-inch jelly-roll pan with 1 tablespoon oil. Punch down dough. Turn out dough onto lightly floured surface. Flatten into rectangle; roll out almost to size of pan. Place dough in pan; gently press dough to edges of pan. Poke surface of dough with end of wooden spoon handle, making indentations every 1 or 2 inches. Brush with remaining 3 tablespoons oil. Gently press peppers and olives into dough, forming decorative pattern. Cover with towel; let rise in warm place 30 minutes or until doubled in bulk.

Preheat oven to 450°F. Bake 12 to 15 minutes or until golden brown. Cut into squares or rectangles. Serve hot.

Makes 12 servings

This thin, chewy bread is originally from Genoa, Italy. Focaccia is almost always rustically shaped in a shallow rectangular pan or in a thin round loaf. It is traditionally brushed with olive oil and sprinkled with salt before baking.

Focaccia

Caponata

1 medium eggplant (about 1 pound), peeled and cut into ½-inch pieces
1 can (14½ ounces) diced Italian plum tomatoes, undrained
1 medium onion, chopped
1 red bell pepper, cut into ½-inch pieces
½ cup medium-hot salsa
¼ cup extra-virgin olive oil
2 tablespoons capers, drained
2 tablespoons balsamic vinegar
3 cloves garlic, minced
1 teaspoon dried oregano leaves
¼ teaspoon salt
⅓ cup packed fresh basil, cut into thin strips
Toasted sliced Italian or French bread

Slow Cooker Directions

Mix all ingredients except basil and bread in slow cooker. Cover and cook on LOW 7 to 8 hours or until vegetables are crisp-tender. Stir in basil. Serve at room temperature on toasted bread.

Makes about 5¼ cups

Caponata

Sesame Italian Breadsticks

- **¼ cup grated Parmesan cheese**
- **3 tablespoons sesame seeds**
- **2 teaspoons Italian seasoning**
- **1 teaspoon kosher salt (optional)**
- **12 frozen bread dough dinner rolls, thawed**
- **¼ cup butter, melted**

1. Preheat oven to 425°F. Spray large baking sheet with nonstick cooking spray.

2. In small bowl, combine cheese, sesame seeds, Italian seasoning and salt, if desired. Spread out on plate.

3. On lightly floured surface, roll each dinner roll into rope, about 8 inches long and ½ inch thick. Place on baking sheet and brush tops and sides with butter. Roll each buttered rope in cheese mixture, pressing mixture into sides. Return ropes to baking sheet, placing 2 inches apart. Twist each rope 3 times, pressing both ends of rope down on baking sheet. Bake 10 to 12 minutes, or until golden brown. *Makes 12 breadsticks*

Toasted Pesto Rounds

- **¼ cup thinly sliced fresh basil or chopped fresh dill**
- **¼ cup (4 ounces) grated Parmesan cheese**
- **1 medium clove garlic, minced**
- **3 tablespoons reduced-fat mayonnaise**
- **12 French bread slices, about ¼ inch thick**
- **4 teaspoons chopped tomato**
- **1 green onion with top, sliced**
- **Black pepper**

1. Preheat broiler.

2. Combine basil, cheese, garlic and mayonnaise in small bowl; mix well.

3. Arrange bread slices in single layer on large nonstick baking sheet or broiler pan. Broil, 6 to 8 inches from heat, 30 to 45 seconds or until bread slices are lightly toasted.

4. Turn bread slices over; spread evenly with basil mixture. Broil 1 minute or until lightly browned. Top evenly with tomato and green onion. Season to taste with pepper. Transfer to serving plate. *Makes 12 servings*

Sesame Italian Bread Sticks

Tomato-Artichoke Focaccia

- **1 package (16 ounces) hot roll mix**
- **2 tablespoons wheat bran**
- **1¼ cups hot water**
- **4 teaspoons olive oil, divided**
- **1 cup thinly sliced onions**
- **2 cloves garlic, minced**
- **1 cup rehydrated sun-dried tomatoes (4 ounces dry), cut into strips**
- **1 cup artichoke hearts, sliced**
- **1 tablespoon minced fresh rosemary**
- **2 tablespoons freshly grated Parmesan cheese**

1. Preheat oven to 400°F. Combine dry ingredients and yeast packet from hot roll mix in large bowl. Add bran; mix well. Stir in hot water and 2 teaspoons oil. Knead dough about 5 minutes or until ingredients are blended.

2. Spray 15½×11½-inch baking pan or 14-inch pizza pan with nonstick cooking spray. Press dough onto bottom of prepared pan. Cover; let rise 15 minutes.

3. Heat 1 teaspoon oil in medium skillet over low heat. Add onions and garlic; cook and stir 2 to 3 minutes or until onions are tender.

4. Brush surface of dough with remaining teaspoon oil. Top dough with onion mixture, tomatoes, artichokes and fresh rosemary. Sprinkle with Parmesan.

5. Bake 25 to 30 minutes or until lightly browned on top. Cut into squares. Garnish each square with fresh rosemary sprigs, if desired.

Makes 16 servings

Pizza Romano

- **1 (10-inch) prepared pizza crust *or* 4 rounds pita bread**
- **1 cup (4 ounces) shredded mozzarella cheese**
- **4 slices HILLSHIRE FARM® Ham, cut into ½-inch strips**
- **1 jar (8 ounces) marinated sun-dried tomatoes, drained (optional)**
- **1 jar (6 ounces) oil-packed artichokes, drained and cut into eighths**
- **1 jar (4 ounces) roasted red peppers, drained and cut into strips**

Preheat oven to 425°F.

Place pizza crust on cookie sheet; top with remaining ingredients. Bake on lower rack of oven 15 to 20 minutes or until crust begins to brown lightly and cheese is melted.

Makes 4 servings

Tomato-Artichoke Focaccia

Italian-Topped Garlic Bread

- 1 pound BOB EVANS® Italian Roll Sausage
- 1 (1-pound) loaf crusty Italian bread
- ½ cup butter, melted
- 2 teaspoons minced garlic
- 2 cups (8 ounces) shredded mozzarella cheese
- 2 cups diced tomatoes
- 8 ounces fresh mushrooms, sliced
- 3 tablespoons grated Parmesan cheese

Preheat oven to 325°F. Crumble and cook sausage in medium skillet until browned. Drain off any drippings. Cut bread into 1-inch slices. Combine butter and garlic in small bowl; brush bread slices with mixture. Arrange on ungreased baking sheet. Combine mozzarella cheese, tomatoes, mushrooms, Parmesan cheese and sausage; spread on bread slices. Bake 10 to 12 minutes or until cheese is melted and golden brown. Serve warm. Refrigerate leftovers.

Makes about 10 appetizer servings

Caponata Spread

- 1½ tablespoons BERTOLLI® Olive Oil
- 1 medium eggplant, diced (about 4 cups)
- 1 medium onion, chopped
- 1½ cups water
- 1 envelope LIPTON® RECIPE SECRETS® Savory Herb with Garlic Soup Mix
- 2 tablespoons chopped fresh parsley (optional)
- Salt and ground black pepper to taste
- Pita chips or thinly sliced Italian or French bread

In 10-inch nonstick skillet, heat oil over medium heat and cook eggplant with onion 3 minutes. Add ½ cup water. Reduce heat to low and simmer covered 3 minutes. Stir in soup mix blended with remaining 1 cup water. Bring to a boil over high heat. Reduce heat to low and simmer uncovered, stirring occasionally, 20 minutes. Stir in parsley, salt and pepper. Serve with pita chips.

Makes about 4 cups spread

Italian-Topped Garlic Bread

Quattro Formaggio Pizza

1 (12-inch) Italian bread shell
½ cup prepared pizza or marinara sauce
4 ounces shaved or thinly sliced provolone cheese
1 cup (4 ounces) shredded smoked or regular mozzarella cheese
2 ounces Asiago or brick cheese, thinly sliced
¼ cup freshly grated Parmesan or Romano cheese

1. Heat oven to 450°F.

2. Place bread shell on baking sheet. Spread pizza sauce evenly over bread shell.

3. Top sauce with provolone, mozzarella, Asiago and Parmesan cheese.

4. Bake 14 minutes or until bread shell is golden brown and cheese is melted.

5. Cut into wedges; serve immediately. *Makes 4 servings*

Serving suggestion: Serve with a tossed green salad.

Prep and Cook Time: 26 minutes

Lasagna Roll-Ups

8 dry lasagne noodles
1 pound Italian sausage
1 cup (1 small) chopped onion
3 cans (6 ounces each) CONTADINA® Italian Paste with Roasted Garlic
2 cups water
1 teaspoon dried oregano, crushed
½ teaspoon dried basil, crushed
1 carton (15 ounces) ricotta cheese
1 package (10 ounces) frozen chopped spinach, thawed, squeezed dry
1½ cups (6 ounces) shredded mozzarella cheese, divided
1 cup (4 ounces) grated Parmesan cheese
1 egg
½ teaspoon salt
¼ teaspoon black pepper

1. Cook pasta according to package directions; drain and keep warm.

2. Crumble sausage into large skillet; add onion. Cook over medium-high heat for 4 to 5 minutes or until sausage is no longer pink; drain.

3. Stir in tomato paste, water, oregano and basil; bring to boil. Reduce heat to low; cook, covered, for 20 minutes.

4. Combine ricotta cheese, spinach, 1 cup mozzarella cheese, Parmesan cheese, egg, salt and pepper in large bowl. Spread about ½ cup cheese mixture onto each noodle; roll up. Place seam-side down in 13×9-inch baking dish. Pour sauce over rolls. Sprinkle with remaining mozzarella cheese.

5. Bake, covered, in preheated 350°F oven for 30 to 40 minutes or until heated through and cheese is melted.

Makes 8 servings

Prep Time: 40 minutes
Cook Time: 40 minutes

Quattro Formaggio Pizza

Herbed Croutons with Savory Bruschetta

- **½ cup regular or reduced fat mayonnaise**
- **¼ cup *French's*® Napa Valley Style Dijon Mustard**
- **1 tablespoon finely chopped green onion**
- **1 clove garlic, minced**
- **¾ teaspoon dried oregano leaves**
- **1 long thin loaf (18 inches) French bread, cut crosswise into ½-inch-thick slices**
- **Savory Bruschetta (recipe follows)**

Combine mayonnaise, mustard, onion, garlic and oregano in small bowl; mix well. Spread herbed mixture on one side of each slice of bread.

Place bread, spread sides up, on grid. Grill over medium-low coals 1 minute or until lightly toasted. Spoon Savory Bruschetta onto herbed croutons. Serve warm.

Makes 6 appetizer servings

Leftover croutons may be served with dips or cut up and served in salads.

Prep Time: 10 minutes
Cook Time: 1 minute

Savory Bruschetta

- **1 pound ripe plum tomatoes, cored, seeded and chopped**
- **1 cup finely chopped fennel bulb or celery**
- **¼ cup chopped fresh basil leaves**
- **3 tablespoons *French's*® Napa Valley Style Dijon Mustard**
- **3 tablespoons olive oil**
- **3 tablespoons balsamic vinegar**
- **2 cloves garlic, minced**
- **½ teaspoon salt**

Combine ingredients in medium bowl; toss well to coat evenly.

Makes 3 cups

Prep Time: 15 minutes

Herbed Croutons with Savory Bruschetta

Easy Taco Dip

- ½ pound ground chuck
- 1 cup frozen corn
- ½ cup chopped onion
- ½ cup salsa
- ½ cup mild taco sauce
- 1 can (4 ounces) diced mild green chilies
- 1 can (4 ounces) sliced ripe olives, drained
- 1 cup (4 ounces) shredded Mexican blend cheese
- Tortilla chips
- Sour cream

Slow Cooker Directions

1. Cook meat in large nonstick skillet over medium-high until no longer pink, stirring to separate; drain. Spoon into slow cooker.

2. Add corn, onion, salsa, taco sauce, chilies and olives to slow cooker; stir to combine. Cover; cook on LOW 2 to 4 hours.

3. Just before serving, stir in cheese. Serve with tortilla chips and sour cream.

Makes about 3 cups dip

Tip: To keep this dip hot through your entire party, simply leave it in the slow cooker on LOW.

Prep Time: 15 minutes
Cook Time: 2 to 4 hours

Easy Taco Dip

Wild Wedges

- 2 (8-inch) fat-free flour tortillas
- Nonstick cooking spray
- 1/3 cup shredded reduced-fat Cheddar cheese
- 1/3 cup chopped cooked chicken or turkey
- 1 green onion, thinly sliced (about 1/4 cup)
- 2 tablespoons mild, thick and chunky salsa

1. Heat large nonstick skillet over medium heat until hot.

2. Spray one side of one flour tortilla with nonstick cooking spray; place sprayed side down in skillet. Top with cheese, chicken, green onion and salsa. Place remaining tortilla over mixture; spray with nonstick cooking spray.

3. Cook 2 to 3 minutes per side or until golden brown and cheese is melted. Cut into 8 triangles. *Makes 4 servings*

Variation: For bean quesadillas, omit the chicken and spread 1/3 cup canned fat-free refried beans over one of the tortillas.

Spanish Potato Omelet

- 1/4 cup olive oil
- 1/4 cup vegetable oil
- 1 pound unpeeled red or white potatoes, cut into 1/8-inch slices
- 1/2 teaspoon salt, divided
- 1 small onion, cut in half lengthwise, thinly sliced crosswise
- 1/4 cup chopped green bell pepper
- 1/4 cup chopped red bell pepper
- 3 eggs

1. Heat oils in large skillet over medium-high heat. Add potatoes to hot oil. Turn with spatula several times to coat all slices with oil. Sprinkle with 1/4 teaspoon of the salt. Cook 6 to 9 minutes or until potatoes become translucent, turning occasionally. Add onion and peppers. Reduce heat to medium. Cook 10 minutes or until potatoes are tender, turning occasionally. Drain mixture in colander placed in large bowl; reserve oil. Let potato mixture stand until cool. Beat eggs with remaining 1/4 teaspoon salt in large bowl. Gently stir in potato mixture; lightly press into bowl until mixture is covered with eggs. Let stand 15 minutes.

2. Heat 2 teaspoons reserved oil in 6-inch nonstick skillet over medium-high heat. Spread potato mixture in pan to form solid layer. Cook until egg on bottom and side of pan has set but top still looks moist. Cover pan with plate. Flip omelet onto plate, then slide omelet back into pan. Continue to cook until bottom is lightly browned. Slide omelet onto serving plate. Let stand 30 minutes before serving. Serve in wedges.

Makes 8 servings

Wild Wedges

Magic Fried Oysters

6 dozen medium to large shucked oysters in their liquor (about 3 pounds)
3 tablespoons Chef Paul Prudhomme's Seafood Magic®, in all
1 cup all-purpose flour
1 cup corn flour
1 cup cornmeal
Vegetable oil for deep-frying

Place oysters and oyster liquor in large bowl. Add 2 tablespoons of the Seafood Magic® to oysters, stirring well. In medium bowl, combine flour, corn flour, cornmeal and the remaining Seafood Magic®. Heat 2 inches or more of oil in deep-fryer or large saucepan to 375°F. Drain oysters and then use a slotted spoon to toss them lightly and quickly in seasoned flour mixture (so oysters don't produce excess moisture, which cakes the flour); shake off excess flour and carefully slip each oyster into hot oil. Fry in single layer in batches just until crispy and golden brown, 1 to 1½ minutes; do not overcook. (Adjust heat as needed to maintain temperature at about 375°F.) Drain on paper towels and serve. *Makes 6 servings*

Bubbling Wisconsin Cheese Bread

½ cup (2 ounces) shredded Wisconsin mozzarella cheese
⅓ cup mayonnaise or salad dressing
⅛ teaspoon garlic powder
⅛ teaspoon onion powder
1 loaf (16 ounces) French bread, halved lengthwise
⅓ cup (1 ounce) grated Wisconsin Parmesan cheese

Preheat oven to 350°F. Combine mozzarella cheese, mayonnaise, garlic powder and onion powder in mixing bowl; mix well (mixture will be very thick). Spread half the mixture over each bread half. Sprinkle half the Parmesan cheese over each half. Bake 20 to 25 minutes or until bubbly and lightly browned.* Cut each half into 8 slices. *Makes 16 servings*

**To broil, position on rack 4 inches from heat for 3 to 5 minutes.*

Favorite recipe from **Wisconsin Milk Marketing Board**

Magic Fried Oysters

Spicy Vegetable Quesadillas

- **1 small zucchini, chopped**
- **½ cup chopped green bell pepper**
- **½ cup chopped onion**
- **2 cloves garlic, minced**
- **½ teaspoon chili powder**
- **½ teaspoon ground cumin**
- **8 (6-inch) flour tortillas**
- **1 cup (4 ounces) shredded reduced-fat Cheddar cheese**
- **¼ cup chopped fresh cilantro**

1. Spray large nonstick skillet with cooking spray. Heat over medium heat until hot. Add zucchini, pepper, onion, garlic, chili powder and cumin; cook and stir 3 to 4 minutes or until vegetables are crisp-tender. Remove vegetables and set aside; wipe skillet clean.

2. Spoon vegetable mixture evenly over half of each tortilla. Sprinkle each evenly with cheese and cilantro. Fold each tortilla in half.

3. Spray same skillet with cooking spray. Add tortillas and heat 1 to 2 minutes per side over medium heat or until lightly browned. Cut into thirds before serving. *Makes 8 servings*

Crawfish Egg Rolls

- **2 tablespoons WESSON® Vegetable Oil**
- **2 (8-ounce) bags shredded cabbage mix *or* 1 pound napa cabbage, shredded**
- **½ pound bean sprouts, washed and drained**
- **2 teaspoons seasoned salt**
- **1½ teaspoons garlic powder**
- **1 pound seasoned crawfish tails, plus juices**
- **½ cup LaCHOY® Lite Soy Sauce**
- **WESSON® Vegetable Oil**
- **1 (16-ounce) package egg roll/spring roll wrappers (20 count)**

In large skillet, heat 2 tablespoons Wesson® Oil. Add cabbage and bean sprouts; sauté until tender. While vegetables are sautéing, add seasoned salt and garlic powder. Fold in crawfish with their juices and soy sauce; sauté 2 minutes more. Drain liquid thoroughly from mixture. Fill a large deep-fry pot or electric skillet to half its depth with Wesson® Oil. Heat oil to 350°F. Meanwhile, place ⅓ cup filling into each egg roll wrapper. Roll according to package directions. Working in small batches, fry egg rolls, turning once. Remove from oil and drain on paper towels. *Makes 20 egg rolls*

Tip: Be creative with egg roll fillings. Try sausage, shrimp or even corned beef and cabbage.

Spicy Vegetable Quesadillas

Snappy Shrimp Zingers

- **2 cups finely chopped cooked, shelled shrimp**
- **½ cup all-purpose flour**
- **3 tablespoons finely chopped green onions**
- **3 tablespoons finely chopped red bell pepper**
- **1 tablespoon minced fresh parsley**
- **1 tablespoon fresh lemon juice**
- **2¼ teaspoons GEBHARDT® Hot Pepper Sauce**
- **2 teaspoons Cajun seasoning**
- **½ teaspoon salt**
- **1 egg, slightly beaten**
- **1 cup fine dry bread crumbs**
- **2 cups WESSON® Canola Oil**

In medium bowl, combine *first 9* ingredients, ending with salt; blend well. Add egg and blend until thoroughly combined. (Mixture will be sticky.) Shape mixture into 12 (3×¾-inch) stick-shaped pieces. Gently roll *each* piece in bread crumbs. In a large skillet, heat oil to 325°F. Gently place shrimp sticks into oil and fry until crisp and golden brown. Drain on paper towels. Serve with your favorite dipping sauce or a squeeze of lemon.

Makes about 12 zingers

Cajun Shrimp Wraps

- **½ cup uncooked rice**
- **1 tablespoon BERTOLLI® Olive Oil**
- **1 pound uncooked medium shrimp, peeled and deveined**
- **1 small red onion, chopped**
- **1 tablespoon finely chopped garlic**
- **2 teaspoons Cajun seasoning (optional)**
- **1 cup RAGÚ® Old World Style® Pasta Sauce**
- **8 (8-inch) flour tortillas, warmed**

Cook rice according to package directions.

Meanwhile, in 12-inch skillet, heat oil over medium-high heat and cook shrimp, onion, garlic and Cajun seasoning 3 minutes or until shrimp turn pink. Stir in Ragú® Pasta Sauce; heat through. Stir hot cooked rice into shrimp mixture. Spoon ½ cup filling onto each tortilla; roll and serve. *Makes 8 servings*

Recipe Tip: To peel and devein shrimp, start at the head of the shrimp and use your fingers to peel off the shell. Use a sharp knife to slit the back and lift out the dark vein.

Snappy Shrimp Zingers

Southern Stuffed New Potatoes with Wisconsin Asiago, Ham and Mushrooms

12 small new red-skinned potatoes (1½ to 2 inches diameter)
2 tablespoons butter, melted
1 teaspoon butter
2 ounces cooked ham, chopped
¼ cup chopped onion
1 teaspoon chopped fresh thyme
½ teaspoon finely chopped garlic
4 ounces button mushrooms, chopped
2½ ounces portobello mushrooms, chopped*
2½ ounces oyster mushrooms, stemmed and chopped*
3 tablespoons whipping cream
½ cup (2 ounces) shredded Wisconsin Asiago cheese
Salt
Black pepper
½ cup (2 ounces) shredded Wisconsin Baby Swiss cheese
½ cup (2 ounces) shredded Wisconsin medium white Cheddar cheese
¼ cup chopped fresh parsley

**Substitute 5 ounces button mushrooms for portobello and oyster mushrooms, if desired.*

Preheat oven to 400°F. Cut ¼ inch off each end of potatoes; discard ends. Cut potatoes in half crosswise. In large bowl, stir together potatoes and 2 tablespoons melted butter until potatoes are well coated. Place potatoes on parchment-lined 15×10-inch jelly-roll pan. Bake for 30 to 40 minutes or until fork tender. Let cool slightly. Scoop out potato pulp, leaving thin shells. Reserve potato pulp for another use. Set shells aside.

Melt 1 teaspoon butter in large skillet over medium-high heat. Add ham; cook 2 to 5 minutes or just until ham begins to brown, stirring occasionally. Add onion, thyme and garlic; decrease heat to medium-low. Cook and stir 2 to 3 minutes or until onion is tender. Add mushrooms. Cook 5 to 6 minutes or until liquid is evaporated, stirring occasionally. Add whipping cream; cook 1 minute, stirring constantly, or until cream is thickened. Stir in Asiago cheese. Season to taste with salt and pepper.

Remove skillet from heat. Meanwhile, in medium bowl, combine Baby Swiss and white Cheddar cheeses; set aside. Fill potato shells with mushroom mixture; sprinkle evenly with Swiss and Cheddar cheese mixture. Cover; refrigerate overnight. To bake, allow potatoes to stand at room temperature for 45 minutes. Preheat oven to 400°F. Bake 12 to 15 minutes or until cheeses are melted and lightly browned. Sprinkle with chopped parsley.

Makes 24 appetizers

Favorite recipe from **Wisconsin Milk Marketing Board**

Brandy-Soaked Scallops

1 pound bacon, cut in half crosswise
2 pounds small sea scallops
⅓ cup olive oil
½ cup brandy
2 tablespoons chopped fresh parsley
1 clove garlic, minced
1 teaspoon black pepper
½ teaspoon salt
½ teaspoon onion powder
Salad greens (optional)

1. Wrap one piece bacon around each scallop; secure with wooden toothpicks, if necessary. Place wrapped scallops in 13×9-inch baking dish.

2. Combine oil, brandy, parsley, garlic, pepper, salt and onion powder in small bowl; mix well. Pour over scallops; cover and marinate in refrigerator at least 4 hours.

3. Remove scallops from marinade; discard marinade. Arrange on rack of broiler pan. Broil, 4 inches from heat, 7 to 10 minutes until bacon is brown. Turn over; cook 5 minutes or until scallops are opaque. Remove wooden toothpicks. Arrange over salad greens and garnish, if desired. *Makes 8 servings*

Cajun-Style Chicken Nuggets

1 envelope LIPTON® RECIPE SECRETS® Onion Soup Mix*
½ cup plain dry bread crumbs
1½ teaspoons chili powder
1 teaspoon ground cumin
1 teaspoon dried thyme leaves, crushed (optional)
¼ teaspoon ground red pepper
2 pounds boneless chicken breasts, cut into 1-inch pieces
BERTOLLI® Extra Light Olive Oil
Assorted mustards (optional)

**Also terrific with LIPTON® RECIPE SECRETS® Onion-Mushroom Soup Mix.*

In large bowl, combine soup mix, bread crumbs, chili powder, cumin, thyme and pepper. Dip chicken in bread crumb mixture, coating well.

In 12-inch skillet, heat ½ inch olive oil and cook chicken over medium heat, turning once, until thoroughly cooked; drain on paper towels. Serve warm and, if desired, with assorted mustards. *Makes about 5 dozen nuggets*

Buffalo Chicken Tenders

3 tablespoons Louisiana-style hot sauce
½ teaspoon paprika
¼ teaspoon ground red pepper
1 pound chicken tenders
½ cup fat-free blue cheese dressing
¼ cup reduced-fat sour cream
2 tablespoons crumbled blue cheese
1 medium red bell pepper, cut into ½-inch slices

1. Preheat oven to 375°F. Combine hot sauce, paprika and ground red pepper in small bowl; brush on all surfaces of chicken. Place chicken in greased 11×7-inch baking dish. Cover; marinate in refrigerator 30 minutes.

2. Bake, uncovered, about 15 minutes or until chicken is no longer pink in center.

3. Combine blue cheese dressing, sour cream and blue cheese in small serving bowl. Garnish as desired. Serve with chicken and bell pepper for dipping. *Makes 10 servings*

Santa Fe Shrimp Martini Cocktails

1 jar (16 ounces) mild salsa
1 ripe small avocado, peeled and chopped
1 tablespoon *Frank's*® RedHot® Cayenne Pepper Sauce
1 tablespoon lime juice
1 tablespoon chopped fresh cilantro leaves
1 pound large shrimp, cooked, peeled and deveined
1 cup *French's*® French Fried Onions
1 lime, cut into 6 wedges

1. Combine salsa, avocado, ***Frank's RedHot*** Sauce, lime juice and cilantro in large bowl. Alternately layer shrimp and salsa mixture in 6 margarita or martini glasses.

2. Microwave French Fried Onions on HIGH for 1 minute until golden. Sprinkle over shrimp. Garnish with lime wedges.
Makes 6 servings

Quick Tip: Purchase cooked, cleaned shrimp from the seafood section of your local supermarket.

Prep Time: 10 minutes
Cook Time: 1 minute

Buffalo Chicken Tenders

Tex-Mex Spring Rolls

2 tablespoons vegetable oil
4 large green onions, finely chopped
1 small red bell pepper, seeded and finely chopped
5 cups shredded Romaine or iceberg lettuce
½ cup drained and rinsed canned black beans
½ cup frozen corn
¼ cup chopped fresh cilantro
3 tablespoons *Frank's® RedHot®* Cayenne Pepper Sauce
1 teaspoon ground cumin
½ cup (2 ounces) shredded Monterey Jack cheese
12 to 15 spring roll wrappers (6 inches), thawed if frozen*
Nonstick cooking spray
Creamy Corn Salsa (recipe page 34)

**Available from Asian markets or in the produce section of larger supermarkets.*

1. Heat oil in large nonstick skillet over medium heat. Add green onions and bell pepper; cook and stir 2 minutes or until tender. Stir in lettuce, beans, corn, cilantro, ***Frank's RedHot*** Sauce and cumin. Cook 3 to 5 minutes or until liquid has evaporated, stirring occasionally. Cool 15 minutes. Stir in cheese.

2. Preheat oven to 400°F. Grease large baking sheet.

3. Place 1 wrapper on work surface like a diamond, with corner at bottom, keeping remaining wrappers covered with plastic wrap. Place about 2 tablespoons filling across center. Brush edges of wrapper with cold water. Fold bottom corner of wrapper up over filling. Fold in and overlap the opposite right and left corners to form log. Continue rolling tightly up. Repeat with remaining wrappers and filling.

4. Place rolls on prepared baking sheet. Lightly spray rolls with cooking spray. Bake 15 minutes or until golden brown and crispy, turning halfway through baking time. Prepare Creamy Corn Salsa; serve warm with spring rolls.

Makes about 12 spring rolls

Cilantro can be found near the lettuce in the produce section of most larger supermarkets. It's flavor complements spicy foods.

Tex-Mex Spring Rolls and Creamy Corn Salsa (page 34)

Hot Hush Puppies

WESSON® Vegetable Oil
1¾ cups cornmeal
½ cup all-purpose flour
1 teaspoon sugar
¾ teaspoon baking soda
½ teaspoon salt
½ teaspoon garlic salt
½ cup diced onion
½ to 1 (4-ounce) can diced jalapeño peppers
1 cup buttermilk
1 egg, beaten

Fill a large deep-fry pot or electric skillet to half its depth with Wesson® Oil. Heat oil to 400°F. Meanwhile, in a large bowl, sift together cornmeal, flour, sugar, baking soda, salt and garlic salt; blend well. Add onion and jalapeño peppers; stir until well blended. In small bowl, combine buttermilk and egg; add to dry ingredients. Stir until batter is moist and *all* ingredients are combined. Working in small batches, carefully drop batter by heaping tablespoons into hot oil. Fry until golden brown, turning once during frying. Remove and drain on paper towels. Serve with your favorite salsa or dipping sauce.

Makes 36 hush puppies

Devilish Eggs

12 hard-cooked eggs, peeled and sliced in half lengthwise
¼ cup nonfat yogurt
2 tablespoons mayonnaise
3 teaspoons fresh lemon juice
2 teaspoons Dijon mustard
1 teaspoon TABASCO® brand Pepper Sauce
½ cup finely chopped fresh herbs (such as parsley, basil, dill or chives)
Salt to taste
Fresh dill or chopped fresh chives (optional)

Remove yolks and place in bowl of food processor with yogurt, mayonnaise, lemon juice, mustard and TABASCO® Sauce; process until smooth. Stir in herbs and salt to taste.

Transfer mixture to gallon-size plastic freezer bag and work it into one corner of bag. Hold bag tightly above mixture; twist until mixture is firmly positioned. Using scissors, snip tip of bag. Holding tip over each egg half, twist bag to generously fill empty yolk cavity. Continue until all eggs are filled.

Refrigerate eggs until ready to serve. Garnish each egg with dill sprig or chopped chives, if desired. *Makes 24 halves*

Hot Hush Puppies

Buffalo Chicken Wings

- **24 chicken wings**
- **1 teaspoon salt**
- **¼ teaspoon ground black pepper**
- **4 cups vegetable oil for frying**
- **¼ cup butter or margarine**
- **¼ cup hot pepper sauce**
- **1 teaspoon white wine vinegar**
- **Celery sticks**
- **1 bottle (8 ounces) blue cheese dressing**

Cut tips off wings at first joint; discard tips. Cut remaining wings into two parts at the joint; sprinkle with salt and pepper. Heat oil in deep fryer or heavy saucepan to 375°F. Add half the wings; fry about 10 minutes or until golden brown and crisp, stirring occasionally. Remove with slotted spoon; drain on paper towels. Repeat with remaining wings.

Melt butter in small saucepan over medium heat; stir in pepper sauce and vinegar. Cook until thoroughly heated. Place wings on large platter. Pour sauce over wings. Serve warm with celery and dressing for dipping. *Makes 24 appetizers*

Favorite recipe from **National Chicken Council**

Home-Style Corn Cakes

- **1 cup yellow cornmeal**
- **½ cup all-purpose flour**
- **½ teaspoon baking powder**
- **½ teaspoon baking soda**
- **1 envelope LIPTON® RECIPE SECRETS® Onion Soup Mix***
- **¾ cup buttermilk**
- **1 egg, beaten**
- **1 can (17¼ ounces) cream-style corn**
- **2 ounces roasted red peppers, chopped (about ¼ cup)**
- **Margarine or butter**

**Or, substitute Lipton® RECIPE SECRETS® Golden Onion Soup Mix.*

In large bowl, combine cornmeal, flour, baking powder and baking soda. Blend soup mix with buttermilk, egg, corn and roasted red peppers; stir into cornmeal mixture.

In 12-inch nonstick skillet or on griddle, melt ½ teaspoon margarine over medium heat. Drop ¼ cup batter for each corn cake and cook, turning once, 5 minutes or until cooked through and golden brown. Remove to serving platter and keep warm. Repeat with remaining batter and additional margarine if needed. Serve with sour cream and prepared salsa, if desired. *Makes about 18 corn cakes*

Tip: Leftover corn cakes may be wrapped and frozen. Remove from wrapping and reheat straight from freezer in preheated 350°F oven for 15 minutes.

Buffalo Chicken Wings

Oven-Fried Tex-Mex Onion Rings

- **½ cup plain dry bread crumbs**
- **⅓ cup yellow cornmeal**
- **1½ teaspoons chili powder**
- **⅛ to ¼ teaspoon ground red pepper**
- **⅛ teaspoon salt**
- **1 tablespoon plus 1½ teaspoons margarine, melted**
- **2 medium onions (about 10 ounces), sliced ⅜ inch thick**
- **2 egg whites**

1. Preheat oven to 450°F. Spray large nonstick baking sheet with nonstick cooking spray; set aside.

2. Combine bread crumbs, cornmeal, chili powder, pepper and salt in medium shallow dish; mix well. Stir in margarine and 1 teaspoon water.

3. Separate onion slices into rings. Place egg whites in large bowl; beat lightly. Add onions; toss lightly to coat evenly. Transfer to bread crumb mixture; toss to coat evenly. Place in single layer on prepared baking sheet.

4. Bake 12 to 15 minutes or until onions are tender and coating is crisp.

Makes 6 servings

Orange Maple Sausage Balls

- **1 pound BOB EVANS® Original Recipe Roll Sausage**
- **1 small onion, finely chopped**
- **1 small red or yellow bell pepper, finely chopped**
- **1 egg**
- **2 tablespoons uncooked cream of wheat cereal**
- **½ cup maple syrup or maple-flavored syrup**
- **3 to 5 tablespoons frozen orange juice concentrate, slightly thawed, to taste**

Combine first 5 ingredients in large bowl until well blended. Shape into ¾-inch balls. Cook in large skillet over medium-high heat until browned on all sides and no longer pink in centers. Drain off drippings. Add syrup and orange juice concentrate to sausage mixture. Cook and stir over medium heat 2 to 3 minutes or until thick bubbly syrup forms. Serve hot. Refrigerate leftovers.

Makes about 24 appetizers

Serving Suggestion: Serve on party picks with sautéed mushrooms and water chestnuts. These meatballs would also make an excellent breakfast item; serve with small pancakes.

Oven-Fried Tex-Mex Onion Rings

Southwestern Chili Cheese Empanadas

3/4 cup (3 ounces) finely shredded taco-flavored cheese*
1/3 cup diced green chilies, drained
1 package (15 ounces) refrigerated pie crusts
1 egg
Chili powder

**If taco-flavored cheese is unavailable, toss 3/4 cup shredded marbled Monterey Jack cheese with 1/2 teaspoon chili powder.*

1. Combine cheese and chilies in small bowl.

2. Unfold 1 pastry crust on floured surface. Roll into 13-inch circle. Cut dough into 16 rounds using 3-inch cookie cutter, rerolling scraps as necessary. Repeat with remaining crust to total 32 circles.

3. Spoon 1 teaspoon cheese mixture in center of each dough round. Fold round in half, sealing edge with tines of fork.

4. Place empanadas on wax paper-lined baking sheets; freeze, uncovered, 1 hour or until firm. Place in resealable plastic food storage bags. Freeze up to 2 months.

5. To complete recipe, preheat oven to 400°F. Place frozen empanadas on ungreased baking sheet. Beat egg and 1 tablespoon water in small bowl; brush on empanadas. Sprinkle with chili powder.

6. Bake 12 to 17 minutes or until golden brown. Remove from baking sheet to wire rack to cool. *Makes 32 appetizers*

Serving suggestion: Serve empanadas with salsa and sour cream.

Make-Ahead Time: up to 2 months in freezer
Final Prep Time: 30 minutes

Empanadas are Spanish pastries similar to turnovers. They are often filled with cheese, meat or vegetables.

Southwestern Chili Cheese Empanadas

Fiesta Chicken Nachos

1 tablespoon BERTOLLI® Olive Oil
1 pound boneless, skinless chicken breasts
1 jar (1 pound) RAGÚ® Cheese Creations!® Double Cheddar Sauce
1 bag (9 ounces) tortilla chips
2 green and/or red bell peppers, diced
1 small onion, chopped
1 large tomato, diced

In 12-inch skillet, heat oil over medium-high heat and cook chicken, stirring occasionally, 8 minutes or until thoroughly cooked. Remove from skillet; cut into strips.

In same skillet, combine chicken and Ragú® Cheese Creations! Sauce; heat through.

On serving platter, arrange layer of tortilla chips, then ½ of the sauce mixture, bell peppers, onion and tomato; repeat, ending with tomato. Garnish, if desired, with chopped fresh cilantro and shredded lettuce. *Makes 4 servings*

Recipe Tip: For a spicier dish, add chopped jalapeño peppers or hot pepper sauce to suit your taste.

Swiss Fondue-Wisconsin

2 cups dry white wine
1 tablespoon lemon juice
1 pound Wisconsin Gruyère cheese, shredded
1 pound Wisconsin Fontina cheese, shredded
1 tablespoon arrowroot
2 ounces kirsch
Pinch of ground nutmeg
French bread cubes
Pears, cut into wedges
Apples, cut into wedges

Bring wine and lemon juice to a boil in fondue pot. Reduce heat to low. Toss cheeses with arrowroot. Gradually add to wine mixture, stirring constantly. When cheese is completely melted, stir in kirsch. Sprinkle with nutmeg and serve with French bread cubes, pears and apples. *Makes 6 servings*

Favorite recipe from **Wisconsin Milk Marketing Board**

Fiesta Chicken Nachos

Santa Fe Potato Cakes

3 cups cooked instant mashed potato flakes or leftover unbuttered mashed potatoes
1 can (4 ounces) diced green chiles, drained
⅔ cup cornmeal, divided
3 green onions, sliced
⅓ cup (about 1½ ounces) shredded cheddar cheese
2 eggs, beaten
2 tablespoons chopped fresh cilantro
1 teaspoon chili powder
½ teaspoon LAWRY'S® Seasoned Salt
½ teaspoon LAWRY'S® Seasoned Pepper
2 tablespoons olive oil, divided
Salsa
Dairy sour cream

In large bowl, combine potatoes, chiles, ½ cup cornmeal, onions, cheese, eggs, cilantro, chili powder, Seasoned Salt and Seasoned Pepper; mix well and shape into eight patties. Sprinkle both sides with remaining cornmeal; set aside. In large nonstick skillet, heat 1 tablespoon oil. Add four patties and cook over medium heat 5 to 7 minutes or until golden brown, turning once. Remove from skillet; keep warm. Repeat with remaining oil and patties. Garnish as desired.

Makes 4 servings

Serving Suggestion: Serve with salsa and sour cream.

Southwestern Quesadillas

3 (8-inch) flour tortillas
I CAN'T BELIEVE IT'S NOT BUTTER!® Spray
¼ teaspoon chili powder, divided
⅛ teaspoon ground cumin, divided
1 cup shredded Monterey Jack or cheddar cheese (about 4 ounces)
1 can (4 ounces) chopped green chilies, drained
1 can (2¼ ounces) sliced pitted ripe olives, drained
2 tablespoons chopped cilantro (optional)

Generously spray one side of one tortilla with I Can't Believe It's Not Butter!® Spray. Sprinkle with ½ of the chili powder and cumin. On baking sheet, arrange tortilla spice-side down, then top with ½ of the cheese, chilies, olives and cilantro. Top with second tortilla. Repeat layers, ending with tortilla. Spray top tortilla generously with I Can't Believe It's Not Butter!® Spray, then sprinkle with remaining chili powder and cumin. Grill or broil until tortillas are golden and cheese is melted. Cut in wedges and serve, if desired, with salsa. *Makes 4 servings*

Santa Fe Potato Cakes

Zesty Crab Cakes with Red Pepper Sauce

- ½ pound raw medium shrimp, shelled and deveined
- 1 egg white
- ⅔ cup heavy cream
- 3 tablespoons *Frank's*® *RedHot*® Cayenne Pepper Sauce
- 1 tablespoon *French's*® Worcestershire Sauce
- ¼ teaspoon seasoned salt
- 1 pound crabmeat or imitation crabmeat, flaked (4 cups)
- 1 red or yellow bell pepper, minced
- 2 green onions, minced
- ¼ cup minced parsley
- 1½ cups fresh bread crumbs
- ½ cup corn oil
- Red Pepper Sauce (recipe follows)

1. Place shrimp, egg white, cream, ***Frank's RedHot*** Sauce, Worcestershire and seasoned salt in food processor. Process until mixture is puréed. Transfer to large bowl.

2. Add crabmeat, bell pepper, onion and parsley. Mix with fork until well blended.

3. Shape crabmeat mixture into 12 (½-inch-thick) patties, using about ¼ cup mixture for each. Coat both sides in bread crumbs.

4. Heat oil in large nonstick skillet. Add crab cakes; cook until browned on both sides. Drain on paper towels. Serve with Red Pepper Sauce. *Makes about 1 dozen crab cakes*

Prep Time: 30 minutes
Cook Time: 15 minutes

Red Pepper Sauce

- 1 jar (7 ounces) roasted red peppers, drained
- ¼ cup mayonnaise
- 3 tablespoons *Frank's*® *RedHot*® Cayenne Pepper Sauce
- 2 tablespoons minced onion
- 1 tablespoon *French's*® Bold n' Spicy Brown Mustard
- 1 tablespoon minced parsley
- 1 clove garlic

Place all ingredients in blender or food processor. Cover; process until smooth. *Makes 1 cup sauce*

Cheesy Pepper & Onion Quesadillas

1/3 cup margarine
3 3/4 cups frozen stir-fry vegetable blend (onions, red, yellow and green peppers)
3/4 teaspoon chili powder
1 package (8 ounces) fat-free cream cheese, softened
1 package (8 ounces) fat-free shredded Cheddar cheese
10 (6-inch) flour tortillas

1. Preheat oven to 425°F.

2. Heat margarine in large nonstick skillet over medium heat until melted. Add stir-fry blend and chili powder. Cook and stir until tender. Drain, reserving margarine.

3. Beat cream cheese with electric mixer on medium speed until smooth. Add Cheddar cheese, mixing until blended. Spread 2 tablespoons cheese mixture onto each tortilla; top with pepper mixture. Fold tortillas in half; place on baking sheet. Brush with reserved margarine.

4. Bake 10 minutes. Cut each tortilla in half. Serve warm with salsa, if desired.

Makes 20 appetizers

Prep time: 10 minutes
Cooking time: 10 minutes

Hot & Spicy Buffalo Chicken Wings

1 can (15 ounces) DEL MONTE® Original Sloppy Joe Sauce
1/4 cup thick and chunky salsa, medium
1 tablespoon red wine vinegar or cider vinegar
20 chicken wings (about 4 pounds)

1. Preheat oven to 400°F.

2. Combine sloppy joe sauce, salsa and vinegar in small bowl. Remove 1/4 cup sauce mixture to serve with cooked chicken wings; cover and refrigerate. Set aside remaining sauce mixture.

3. Arrange wings in single layer in large, shallow baking pan; brush wings with remaining sauce mixture.

4. Bake chicken, uncovered, on middle rack in oven 35 minutes or until chicken is no longer pink in center, turning and brushing with remaining sauce mixture after 15 minutes. Serve with reserved 1/4 cup sauce. Garnish, if desired.

Makes 4 servings

Prep Time: 5 minutes
Cook Time: 35 minutes

Asian Openers

Oriental Chicken Wings

32 pieces chicken wing drums and flats
1 cup chopped red onion
1 cup soy sauce
¾ cup packed light brown sugar
¼ cup dry cooking sherry
2 tablespoons chopped fresh ginger
2 cloves garlic, minced
Chopped fresh chives

Slow Cooker Directions

Preheat broiler. Broil chicken wings about 5 minutes per side. Transfer chicken to slow cooker.

Combine onion, soy sauce, brown sugar, sherry, ginger and garlic in large bowl. Add to slow cooker; stir to combine. Cover and cook on LOW 5 to 6 hours or on HIGH 2 to 3 hours. Sprinkle with chives. *Makes 32 appetizers*

Oriental Chicken Wings

Bean and Vegetable Egg Rolls

- **1 tablespoon sesame seeds**
- **1 tablespoon dark sesame oil**
- **2 green onions with tops, sliced**
- **1 tablespoon minced fresh ginger**
- **2 cloves garlic, minced**
- **2 cups shredded napa cabbage**
- **1 cup shredded carrots**
- **½ cup chopped celery**
- **½ cup chopped mushrooms**
- **4 ounces fresh or canned bean sprouts, rinsed**
- **1 can (15 ounces) chick-peas (garbanzo beans), rinsed and drained**
- **1½ teaspoons reduced-sodium soy sauce**
- **Pepper (optional)**
- **1 egg, beaten**
- **12 egg roll wrappers**
- **Peanut or vegetable oil**
- **Plum Dipping Sauce (recipe follows)**

1. Combine sesame seeds and sesame oil in large skillet. Cook and stir over low heat 2 to 3 minutes or until sesame seeds begin to brown. Add green onions, ginger and garlic; cook and stir 1 to 2 minutes. Add cabbage, carrots, celery, mushrooms and bean sprouts; cover. Cook 8 minutes or until cabbage is wilted. Stir in chick-peas and soy sauce; season to taste with pepper, if desired. Cool 10 minutes; stir in egg.

2. Place ⅓ cup vegetable mixture near one corner of egg roll wrapper. Brush edges of egg roll wrapper with water. Fold bottom corner of egg roll wrapper up over filling; fold sides in and roll up. Repeat with remaining filling and egg roll wrappers.

3. Heat 1 inch peanut oil in large, heavy saucepan over medium-high heat until oil is 375°F; adjust heat to maintain temperature. Fry egg rolls 3 to 5 minutes or until golden. Drain on paper towels; serve hot with Plum Dipping Sauce. Garnish, if desired.

Makes 12 servings

Plum Dipping Sauce

- **⅔ cup plum sauce**
- **3 tablespoons reduced-sodium soy sauce**
- **2 tablespoons rice wine vinegar or cider vinegar**
- **1 tablespoon grated fresh ginger**
- **1 tablespoon honey**
- **2 green onions with tops, sliced**
- **3 to 4 drops hot chili oil (optional)**

1. Combine all ingredients in medium bowl; mix well. Cover; refrigerate until ready to serve.

Makes about 1 cup

Cook's Tip: While preparing egg rolls, keep unused egg roll wrappers covered with a damp towel to prevent drying out.

Bean and Vegetable Egg Rolls

Savory Chicken Satay

1 envelope LIPTON® RECIPE SECRETS® Onion Soup Mix
1/4 cup BERTOLLI® Olive Oil
2 tablespoons firmly packed brown sugar
2 tablespoons SKIPPY® Peanut Butter
1 pound boneless, skinless chicken breasts, pounded and cut into thin strips
12 to 16 wooden skewers, soaked in water

1. In large plastic bag, combine soup mix, oil, brown sugar and peanut butter. Add chicken and toss to coat well. Close bag and marinate in refrigerator 30 minutes.

2. Remove chicken from marinade, discarding marinade. On large skewers, thread chicken, weaving back and forth.

3. Grill or broil chicken until chicken is thoroughly cooked. Serve with your favorite dipping sauces.

Makes 12 to 16 appetizers

Prep Time: 15 minutes
Marinate Time: 30 minutes
Cook Time: 8 minutes

Sesame Chicken Salad Wonton Cups

Nonstick cooking spray
20 (3-inch) wonton wrappers
1 tablespoon sesame seeds
2 small boneless skinless chicken breasts (about 8 ounces)
1 cup fresh green beans, cut diagonally into 1/2-inch pieces
1/4 cup reduced-fat mayonnaise
1 tablespoon chopped fresh cilantro (optional)
2 teaspoons honey
1 teaspoon reduced-sodium soy sauce
1/8 teaspoon ground red pepper

1. Preheat oven to 350°F. Spray miniature muffin pan with nonstick cooking spray. Press 1 wonton wrapper into each muffin cup; spray with nonstick cooking spray. Bake 8 to 10 minutes or until golden brown. Cool in pan on wire rack before filling.

2. Place sesame seeds in shallow baking pan. Bake 5 minutes or until lightly toasted, stirring occasionally. Set aside to cool.

3. Meanwhile, bring 2 cups water to a boil in medium saucepan. Add chicken. Reduce heat to low; cover. Simmer 10 minutes or until chicken is no longer pink in center, adding green beans after 7 minutes. Drain.

4. Finely chop chicken. Place in medium bowl. Add green beans and remaining ingredients; mix lightly. Spoon lightly rounded tablespoonful of chicken mixture into each wonton cup. Garnish, if desired.

Makes 10 servings

Savory Chicken Satay

Thai-Style Pork Kabobs

- **1/3 cup reduced-sodium soy sauce**
- **2 tablespoons fresh lime juice**
- **2 tablespoons water**
- **2 teaspoons hot chili oil***
- **2 cloves garlic, minced**
- **1 teaspoon minced fresh ginger**
- **12 ounces well-trimmed pork tenderloin**
- **1 red or yellow bell pepper, cut into 1/2-inch chunks**
- **1 red or sweet onion, cut into 1/2-inch chunks**
- **2 cups hot cooked rice**

**If hot chili oil is not available, combine 2 teaspoons vegetable oil and 1/2 teaspoon red pepper flakes in small microwavable cup. Microwave at HIGH 1 minute. Let stand 5 minutes to infuse flavor.*

1. Combine soy sauce, lime juice, water, chili oil, garlic and ginger in medium bowl; reserve 1/3 cup mixture for dipping sauce. Set aside.

2. Cut pork tenderloin lengthwise in half; cut crosswise into 4-inch slices. Cut slices into 1/2-inch strips. Add to bowl with soy sauce mixture; toss to coat. Cover; refrigerate at least 30 minutes or up to 2 hours, turning once.

3. To prevent sticking, spray grid with nonstick cooking spray. Prepare coals for grilling.

4. Remove pork from marinade; discard marinade. Alternately weave pork strips and thread bell pepper and onion chunks onto eight 8- to 10-inch metal skewers.

5. Grill, covered, over medium-hot coals 6 to 8 minutes or until pork is no longer pink in center, turning halfway through grilling time. Serve with rice and reserved dipping sauce.

Makes 4 servings

Beef and Lettuce Bundles

- **1 pound ground beef**
- **1/2 cup sliced green onions**
- **1 medium clove garlic, minced**
- **2/3 cup chopped water chestnuts**
- **1/2 cup chopped red bell pepper**
- **1 tablespoon soy sauce**
- **1 tablespoon seasoned rice vinegar**
- **2 tablespoons chopped fresh cilantro**
- **1 or 2 heads leaf lettuce, separated into leaves (discard outer leaves)**
- **Hoisin sauce (optional)**

Brown ground beef in medium skillet. Drain. Add onions and garlic. Cook until tender. Stir in water chestnuts, red pepper, soy sauce and vinegar. Cook, stirring occasionally, until red pepper is crisp-tender and most of liquid evaporates.

Stir in cilantro. Spoon ground beef mixture onto lettuce leaves; sprinkle with hoisin sauce, if desired. Wrap lettuce leaf around ground beef mixture to make appetizer bundle.

Makes 8 appetizer servings

Thai-Style Pork Kabobs

Spicy Apricot Sesame Wings

- 1/3 cup ***Frank's® RedHot®*** **Cayenne Pepper Sauce**
- 1/2 cup ***French's®*** **Napa Valley Style Dijon Mustard**
- **2 tablespoons Oriental sesame oil**
- **1 tablespoon red wine vinegar**
- **1/2 cup apricot jam**
- **2 pounds chicken wings, split and tips discarded**
- **2 tablespoons toasted sesame seeds***

**To toast sesame seeds, place on baking sheet and bake at 375°F 8 to 10 minutes or until golden.*

1. Stir ***Frank's RedHot*** Sauce, mustard, sesame oil and vinegar in small measuring cup. Spoon 1/4 cup ***Frank's RedHot*** Sauce mixture and apricot jam into blender or food processor. Cover; process until smooth. Reserve for basting and dipping sauce.

2. Place wings in large bowl. Pour remaining ***Frank's RedHot*** Sauce mixture over wings; toss to coat. Cover; marinate in refrigerator 20 minutes.

3. Place wings on oiled grid and discard any remaining marinade. Grill over medium heat 25 to 30 minutes or until crispy and no longer pink, turning often. Brush with 1/4 cup of the sauce during last 10 minutes of cooking. Place wings on serving platter; sprinkle with sesame seeds. Serve with remaining sauce. *Makes 8 servings*

Prep Time: 15 minutes
Marinate Time: 20 minutes
Cook Time: 25 minutes

Chili Garlic Prawns

- **2 tablespoons vegetable oil**
- **1 pound prawns, peeled and deveined**
- **3 tablespoons LEE KUM KEE® Chili Garlic Sauce**
- **1 green onion, cut into slices**

1. Heat oil in wok or skillet.

2. Add prawns and stir-fry until just pink.

3. Add chili garlic sauce and stir-fry until prawns are completely cooked.

4. Sprinkle with green onion and serve. *Makes 4 servings*

Spicy Apricot Sesame Wings

Pearl-Rice Balls

½ cup sweet (glutinous) rice
2 to 3 drops yellow food coloring (optional)
3 large dried black Asian mushrooms
Boiling water
½ pound lean ground pork or beef
1 small egg white, lightly beaten
1 tablespoon minced green onion, white part only
1½ teaspoons soy sauce
1½ teaspoons rice wine
½ teaspoon minced fresh ginger
½ teaspoon sugar
¼ teaspoon salt
Pinch black pepper
1½ teaspoons cornstarch

Garlic-Soy Sauce

3 tablespoons soy sauce
1½ tablespoons white vinegar
¼ teaspoon minced garlic
⅛ teaspoon sugar

1. To prepare Pearl-Rice Balls, place rice in medium bowl of cold water. Comb through rice with fingers several times; drain. Repeat until water remains clear. Return rice to bowl; fill with warm tap water. Stir in food coloring. Soak rice 3 to 4 hours, or refrigerate, covered, overnight. Drain.

2. Place mushrooms in bowl and cover with boiling water. Let stand 30 minutes. Drain. Remove and discard stems; squeeze out excess water. Mince mushrooms. Combine with pork, egg white, green onion, soy sauce, rice wine, ginger, sugar, salt and pepper in bowl; mix well. Stir in cornstarch.

3. Shape meat mixture into 1-inch balls; mixture will be fairly soft. Roll each ball in rice to coat completely; press lightly between hands to make rice adhere.*

4. Place 12-inch bamboo steamer in wok. Add water to ½ inch below steamer. (Water should not touch steamer.) Remove steamer. Bring water to a boil over high heat.

5. Place pearl-rice balls in single layer in steamer lined with wet cloth, leaving about ½-inch space between balls; cover. Place steamer in wok. Steam, covered, over high heat 40 minutes until rice is tender, adding boiling water as needed to maintain water level.

6. To prepare Garlic-Soy Sauce, mix ingredients in small bowl.

7. Transfer Pearl-Rice Balls from steamer to serving dish. Serve with Garlic-Soy Sauce. *Makes about 18 balls*

**Pearl-Rice Balls can be made through Step 3 up to 8 hours ahead. Refrigerate, covered with plastic wrap; uncover and let stand at room temperature 15 to 20 minutes before steaming. Recipe can be doubled if you have 2 steamer baskets.*

Crisp Fish Cakes

Ginger Dipping Sauce (recipe follows)
1 pound boneless catfish, halibut or cod fillets, cut into 1-inch pieces
1 tablespoon fish sauce
3 cloves garlic, minced
1 tablespoon chopped fresh cilantro
2 teaspoons grated lemon peel
1 teaspoon finely chopped fresh ginger
⅛ teaspoon ground red pepper
Peanut oil for frying
1 head curly leaf lettuce
1 medium green or red apple, cut into thin strips *or* 1 ripe mango, diced
½ cup fresh cilantro
⅓ cup fresh mint

1. Prepare Ginger Dipping Sauce; set aside.

2. Process fish pieces in food processor 10 to 20 seconds or just until coarsely chopped. (Do not purée.) Add fish sauce, garlic, chopped cilantro, lemon peel, ginger and red pepper; process 5 seconds or until combined.

3. Rub cutting board with 1 to 2 teaspoons oil. Place fish mixture on board; pat evenly into 7-inch square. Cut into 16 squares; shape each square into 2-inch patty.

4. Heat 1 to 1½ inches oil in Dutch oven or large skillet over medium-high heat until oil registers 360°F to 375°F on deep-fry thermometer. Place 4 patties on slotted spoon and lower into hot oil.

5. Fry patties 2 to 3 minutes or until golden and fish is white in center. (Overcooking will dry fish and cause patties to shrink.) Remove with slotted spoon to paper towels; drain. Repeat with remaining patties, returning oil to 360°F to 375°F before adding new batch.

6. Pile fish cakes on serving platter with lettuce leaves, apple, cilantro leaves, mint and Ginger Dipping Sauce. To eat, stack 1 fish cake, apple strips, cilantro and mint in center of lettuce leaf. Drizzle with sauce; enclose filling in lettuce leaf and eat out of hand.

Makes 6 to 8 servings

Ginger Dipping Sauce

¼ cup rice vinegar
2 tablespoons water
1 teaspoon sugar
1 teaspoon finely chopped fresh ginger
½ teaspoon red pepper flakes
½ teaspoon fish sauce

Combine all ingredients in small bowl; stir until sugar dissolves.

Makes about ⅓ cup

Sesame Portobello Mushrooms

4 large portobello mushrooms
2 tablespoons sweet rice wine
2 tablespoons reduced-sodium soy sauce
2 cloves garlic, minced
1 teaspoon dark sesame oil

1. Remove and discard stems from mushrooms; set caps aside. Combine remaining ingredients in small bowl.

2. Brush both sides of mushrooms with soy sauce mixture. Grill mushrooms top side up on covered grill over medium coals 3 to 4 minutes. Brush tops with soy sauce mixture and turn over; grill 2 minutes more or until mushrooms are lightly browned. Turn again and grill, basting frequently, 4 to 5 minutes or until tender when pressed with back of spatula. Remove mushrooms and cut diagonally into ½-inch-thick slices.

Makes 4 servings

Beef Soup with Noodles

2 tablespoons soy sauce
1 teaspoon minced fresh ginger
¼ teaspoon red pepper flakes
1 boneless beef top sirloin steak, cut 1 inch thick (about ¾ pound)
1 tablespoon peanut or vegetable oil
2 cups sliced fresh mushrooms
2 cans (about 14 ounces each) beef broth
3 ounces (1 cup) fresh snow peas, cut diagonally into 1-inch pieces
1½ cups hot cooked fine egg noodles (2 ounces uncooked)
1 green onion, cut diagonally into thin slices
1 teaspoon dark sesame oil (optional)
Red bell pepper strips for garnish

1. Combine soy sauce, ginger and red pepper flakes in small bowl. Spread mixture evenly over both sides of steak. Marinate at room temperature 15 minutes.

2. Heat deep skillet over medium-high heat. Add peanut oil; heat until hot. Drain steak; reserve soy sauce mixture (there will only be a small amount of mixture). Add steak to skillet; cook 4 to 5 minutes per side.* Let stand on cutting board 10 minutes.

3. Add mushrooms to skillet; stir-fry 2 minutes. Add broth, snow peas and reserved soy sauce mixture; bring to a boil, scraping up browned meat bits. Reduce heat to medium-low. Stir in noodles.

4. Cut steak across the grain into ⅛-inch slices; cut each slice into 1-inch pieces. Stir into soup; heat through. Stir in onion and sesame oil. Ladle into soup bowls. Garnish with bell pepper strips. *Makes 6 appetizer servings (about 6 cups)*

**Cooking time is for medium-rare doneness. Adjust time for desired doneness.*

Sesame Portobello Mushrooms

Gingered Chicken Pot Stickers

- **3 cups finely shredded cabbage**
- **4 green onions with tops, finely chopped**
- **1 egg white, lightly beaten**
- **1 tablespoon light soy sauce**
- **1 tablespoon minced fresh ginger**
- **¼ teaspoon red pepper flakes**
- **¼ pound ground chicken breast, cooked and drained**
- **24 wonton wrappers, at room temperature**
- **Cornstarch**
- **½ cup water**
- **1 tablespoon oyster sauce**
- **2 teaspoons grated lemon peel**
- **½ teaspoon honey**
- **⅛ teaspoon red pepper flakes**
- **1 tablespoon peanut oil**

Steam cabbage 5 minutes, then cool to room temperature. Squeeze out any excess moisture; set aside. To prepare filling, combine egg white, soy sauce, ¼ teaspoon red pepper, ginger and green onions in large bowl; blend well. Stir in cabbage and chicken.

To prepare pot stickers, place 1 tablespoon filling in center of 1 wonton wrapper. Gather edges around filling, pressing firmly at top to seal. Repeat with remaining wrappers and filling. Place pot stickers on large baking sheet dusted with cornstarch. Refrigerate 1 hour or until cold. Meanwhile, to prepare sauce, combine remaining ingredients except oil in small bowl; mix well. Set aside.

Heat oil in large nonstick skillet over high heat. Add pot stickers and cook until bottoms are golden brown. Pour sauce over top. Cover and cook 3 minutes. Uncover and cook until all liquid is absorbed. Serve warm on tray as finger food or on small plates with chopsticks as first course. *Makes 8 appetizer servings*

Spring Rolls

- **1 cup pre-shredded cabbage or coleslaw mix**
- **½ cup finely chopped cooked ham**
- **¼ cup finely chopped water chestnuts**
- **¼ cup thinly sliced green onions**
- **3 tablespoons plum sauce, divided**
- **1 teaspoon dark sesame oil**
- **3 (6-inch) flour tortillas**

Combine cabbage, ham, water chestnuts, onions, 2 tablespoons plum sauce and sesame oil in medium bowl. Mix well. Spread remaining 1 tablespoon plum sauce evenly over tortillas. Spread about ½ cup cabbage mixture on each tortilla to within ¼ inch of edge; roll up. Wrap each tortilla tightly in plastic wrap. Refrigerate at least 1 hour or up to 24 hours before serving. Cut each tortilla diagonally into 4 pieces. *Makes 12 appetizers*

Gingered Chicken Pot Stickers

Barbecued Ribs

- **3 to 4 pounds lean pork baby back ribs or spareribs**
- **1/3 cup hoisin sauce**
- **4 tablespoons soy sauce, divided**
- **3 tablespoons dry sherry**
- **3 cloves garlic, minced**
- **2 tablespoons honey**
- **1 tablespoon dark sesame oil**

1. Place ribs in large plastic bag. Combine hoisin sauce, 3 tablespoons soy sauce, sherry and garlic in cup; pour over ribs. Close bag securely; turn to coat. Marinate in refrigerator at least 4 hours or up to 24 hours.

2. Preheat oven to 375°F. Drain ribs; reserve marinade. Place ribs on rack in shallow, foil-lined roasting pan. Cook 30 minutes. Turn; brush ribs with half of reserved marinade. Cook 15 minutes. Turn ribs over; brush with remaining marinade. Cook 15 minutes.

3. Combine remaining 1 tablespoon soy sauce, honey and sesame oil in small bowl; brush over ribs. Cook 5 to 10 minutes until ribs are browned and crisp.* Cut into serving-size pieces.

Makes 8 appetizer servings

**Ribs may be made ahead to this point; cover and refrigerate ribs up to 3 days. To reheat ribs, wrap in foil; cook in preheated 350°F oven 40 minutes or until heated through. Cut into serving-size pieces.*

Miniature Teriyaki Pork Kabobs

- **1 pound boneless pork, cut into 4×1×½-inch strips**
- **1 small green bell pepper, cut into 1×¼×¼-inch strips**
- **1 can (11 ounces) mandarin oranges, drained**
- **¼ cup teriyaki sauce**
- **1 tablespoon honey**
- **1 tablespoon vinegar**
- **1/8 teaspoon garlic powder**

Soak 24 (8-inch) bamboo skewers in water 10 minutes. Thread 1 pepper strip, then pork strips accordion-style with mandarin oranges on skewers. Place 1 pepper strip on end of each skewer. Arrange skewers on broiler pan.

For sauce, combine teriyaki sauce, honey, vinegar and garlic powder in small bowl; mix well. Brush sauce over kabobs. Broil, 6 inches from heat, about 15 minutes or until pork is done, turning and basting with sauce occasionally.

Makes about 24 appetizers

Favorite recipe from **National Pork Board**

Barbecued Ribs

Mini Marinated Beef Skewers

1 pound lean beef round tip, cut 1 inch thick
2 tablespoons reduced-sodium soy sauce
1 tablespoon dry sherry
1 teaspoon dark sesame oil
2 cloves garlic, minced
18 cherry tomatoes (optional)

1. Cut beef across the grain into ⅛-inch slices. Place in large resealable plastic food storage bag. Combine soy sauce, sherry, oil and garlic in cup; pour over steak. Seal bag; turn to coat. Marinate in refrigerator at least 30 minutes or up to 2 hours.

2. Soak 18 (6-inch) skewers in water 20 minutes.

3. Drain steak; discard marinade. Weave beef accordion-fashion onto skewers. Place on rack of broiler pan.

4. Broil 4 to 5 inches from heat 2 minutes. Turn skewers over; broil 2 minutes or until beef is barely pink.

5. If desired, garnish each skewer with 1 cherry tomato. Place skewers on lettuce-lined platter. Serve warm.

Makes 6 servings (3 skewers each)

Almond Chicken Cups

1 tablespoon vegetable oil
½ cup chopped red bell pepper
½ cup chopped onion
2 cups chopped cooked chicken
⅔ cup prepared sweet-sour sauce
½ cup chopped almonds
2 tablespoons soy sauce
6 (6- or 7-inch) flour tortillas

1. Preheat oven to 400°F. Heat oil in small skillet over medium heat until hot. Add bell pepper and onion. Cook and stir 3 minutes or until crisp-tender.

2. Combine vegetable mixture, chicken, sweet-sour sauce, almonds and soy sauce in medium bowl; mix until well blended.

3. Cut each tortilla in half. Place each half in 2¾-inch muffin cup. Fill each with about ¼ cup chicken mixture.

4. Bake 8 to 10 minutes or until tortilla edges are crisp and filling is hot. Remove muffin pan to cooling rack. Let stand 5 minutes before serving. *Makes 12 chicken cups*

Prep and Cook Time: 30 minutes

Mini Marinated Beef Skewers

Champagne Punch

1 orange
1 lemon
¼ cup cranberry-flavored liqueur or cognac
¼ cup orange-flavored liqueur or Triple Sec
1 bottle (750 ml) pink or regular champagne or sparkling white wine, well chilled
Fresh cranberries (optional)
Citrus strips for garnish

Remove colored peel, not white pith, from orange and lemon in long thin strips with citrus peeler. Refrigerate orange and lemon for another use. Combine peels and cranberry- and orange-flavored liqueurs in glass pitcher. Cover and refrigerate 2 to 6 hours.

Just before serving, tilt pitcher to one side and slowly pour in champagne. Leave peels in pitcher for added flavor. Place a cranberry in bottom of each glass. Pour into champagne glasses. Garnish with citrus strips tied in knots, if desired.

Makes 4 cups (6 to 8 servings)

Nonalchoholic Cranberry Punch: Pour 3 cups well-chilled club soda into ⅔ cup (6 ounces) cranberry cocktail concentrate, thawed. Makes 3½ cups (6 servings).

Champagne Punch

Citrus Cooler

- 2 cups fresh squeezed orange juice
- 2 cups unsweetened pineapple juice
- 1 teaspoon fresh lemon juice
- ¾ teaspoon vanilla extract
- ¾ teaspoon coconut extract
- 2 cups cold sparkling water

Combine juices and extracts in large pitcher; refrigerate until cold. Stir in sparkling water. Serve over ice.

Makes 9 servings

Lemonade

- 1 cup Time-Saver Sugar Syrup (recipe follows)
- 1⅓ cups squeezed lemon juice
- 4 cups water

Prepare Time-Saver Sugar Syrup. Combine Time-Saver Sugar Syrup, lemon juice and water. Mix thoroughly; serve over ice. Garnish as desired.

Makes 1½ quarts lemonade

Favorite recipe from **The Sugar Association, Inc.**

Time-Saver Sugar Syrup

- 1 cup water
- 2 cups sugar

Combine water and sugar in medium saucepan. Cook and stir over medium heat until sugar dissolves. Cool to room temperature; strain through sieve. Refrigerate until chilled.

Makes about 2 cups syrup

Favorite recipe from **The Sugar Association, Inc.**

Citrus Cooler

Toasted Almond Horchata

3½ cups water, divided
2 (3-inch) cinnamon sticks
1 cup uncooked instant white rice
1 cup slivered almonds, toasted
3 cups cold water
¾ to 1 cup sugar
½ teaspoon vanilla
Lime wedges for garnish

Combine 3 cups water and cinnamon sticks in medium saucepan. Cover and bring to a boil over high heat. Reduce heat to medium-low. Simmer 15 minutes. Remove from heat; let cool to temperature of hot tap water. Measure cinnamon water to equal 3 cups, adding additional hot water if needed.

Place rice in food processor; process using on/off pulsing action 1 to 2 minutes or until rice is powdery. Add almonds; process until finely ground (mixture will begin to stick together). Remove rice mixture to medium bowl; stir in cinnamon water. Let stand 1 hour or until mixture is thick and rice grains are soft.

Remove cinnamon sticks; discard. Pour mixture into food processor. Add remaining ½ cup water; process 2 to 4 minutes or until mixture is very creamy. Strain mixture through fine-meshed sieve or several layers of dampened cheesecloth into half-gallon pitcher. Stir in 3 cups cold water, sugar and vanilla; stir until sugar is completely dissolved.

To serve, pour over ice cubes, if desired. Garnish, if desired.

Makes 8 to 10 servings

Chocolate Root Beer Float

1 tablespoon sugar
2 teaspoons HERSHEY'S Cocoa
1 tablespoon hot water
1 scoop vanilla ice cream
Cold root beer

1. Stir together sugar and cocoa in 12-ounce glass; stir in water.
2. Add ice cream and enough root beer to half fill glass; stir gently. Fill glass with root beer. Stir; serve immediately.

Makes one 12-ounce serving

Toasted Almond Horchata

Bloody Marys

1 quart tomato juice
½ cup vodka
2 tablespoons *Frank's® RedHot®* Cayenne Pepper Sauce
2 tablespoons *French's®* Worcestershire Sauce
2 tablespoons prepared horseradish
1 tablespoon lemon juice
1 teaspoon celery salt

Combine all ingredients in large pitcher; refrigerate. Serve over ice.

Makes 4 servings

Prep Time: 5 minutes
Chill Time: 30 minutes

Pineapple Margarita

⅔ cup DOLE® Pineapple Juice
1½ ounces tequila
1 ounce Triple Sec
Juice of 1 lemon
Crushed ice

• Combine pineapple juice, tequila, Triple Sec and lemon juice in blender. Add ice; blend until slushy. Serve in frosted glasses. (Do not put salt on rim.)

Makes 2 servings

A "virgin" Bloody Mary can be made by omitting the vodka in the above recipe.

Bloody Marys

Piña Colada Punch

5 cups DOLE® Pineapple Juice, divided
1 can (15 ounces) real cream of coconut
1 liter lemon-lime soda
2 limes
1½ cups light rum (optional)
Ice cubes
Mint sprigs

• Chill all ingredients.

• Blend 2 cups pineapple juice with cream of coconut in blender. Combine puréed mixture with remaining 3 cups pineapple juice, soda, juice of 1 lime, rum and ice. Garnish with 1 sliced lime and mint. *Makes 15 servings*

Kahlúa® Brave Bull

1½ ounces KAHLÚA® Liqueur
1½ ounces sanza tequila
Lemon twist for garnish

Pour Kahlúa® and tequila over ice in glass. Stir. Garnish with lemon twist. *Makes 1 serving*

Mimosa Cocktail

1 bottle (750 mL) champagne, chilled
3 cups Florida orange juice, chilled

Combine equal parts of champagne and orange juice in champagne glasses. Serve immediately. *Makes 12 servings*

Favorite recipe from **Florida Department of Citrus**

Piña Colada Punch

Bahama Slush

1 cup DEL MONTE® Tomato Juice, chilled
1 cup DEL MONTE Pineapple Juice, chilled
1 tablespoon lime juice
Crushed ice

1. Combine juices; serve over crushed ice.

Makes 2 (8-ounce) servings

Prep Time: 2 minutes

Citrus Punch

- 2 cups orange juice
- 2 cups grapefruit juice
- ¾ cup lime juice
- ½ cup light corn syrup
- 1 bottle (750 mL) ginger ale, white grape juice, Asti Spumante or sparkling wine

Frozen Fruit Ice

- 4 oranges, sectioned
- 1 to 2 limes, cut into ⅛-inch slices
- 1 lemon, cut into ⅛-inch slices
- 1 pint strawberries, stemmed and halved
- 1 cup raspberries

Combine juices and corn syrup in 2-quart pitcher. Stir until corn syrup dissolves. (Stir in additional corn syrup to taste.) Refrigerate 2 hours or until cold. Stir in ginger ale just before serving.

To prepare Frozen Fruit Ice, spread oranges, limes, lemon, strawberries and raspberries on baking sheet. Freeze 4 hours or until firm.

Divide Frozen Fruit Ice between 8 (12-ounce) glasses or 10 wide-rimmed wine glasses. Fill glasses with punch. Garnish with fresh mint sprigs, if desired. Serve immediately.

Makes 8 to 10 servings (about 5 cups)

Strawberry-Peach Cooler

1 cup sliced strawberries
1 cup chopped peaches
2 tablespoons sugar
1 bottle (750 ml) white wine, chilled
1 bottle (1 quart) sparkling water, chilled
Mint sprigs
Ice

Combine strawberries and peaches in small bowl. Sprinkle with sugar; stir gently. Let stand at room temperature 30 minutes. Pour fruit into punch bowl. Gently pour in wine and water. Add mint sprigs and ice. *Makes about 2 quarts*

Nonalcoholic Cooler: Use only 1 tablespoon sugar. Substitute 1 quart apple juice for wine.

Mojito

6 packets NatraTaste® Brand Sugar Substitute
2 cups very hot water
4 to 6 mint leaves
¼ cup fresh lime juice
2 ounces light or dark rum
½ cup seltzer or club soda
Ice cubes

1. Combine the NatraTaste® and water in a jar or container with a lid, shake.

2. Place the mint leaves in the bottom of two glasses and press down with a spoon to release the flavor. Divide lime juice and rum between glasses. Add ¼ cup *each* sweetened water and seltzer to each glass. Add ice cubes and stir.

Makes 2 servings

Note: Refrigerate remaining sweetened water for future use.

Italian Soda

Ice
3 to 4 tablespoons flavored syrup
2 tablespoons half-and-half (optional)
¾ cup chilled club soda

Fill 12-ounce glass with ice. Add syrup and half-and-half. Pour in club soda and stir. Serve immediately. *Makes 1 serving*

Cranberry Sangría

- **1 bottle (750 ml) Beaujolais or dry red wine**
- **1 cup cranberry juice cocktail**
- **1 cup orange juice**
- **½ cup cranberry-flavored liqueur (optional)**
- **1 orange,* thinly sliced**
- **1 lime,* thinly sliced**

Note: *The orange and lime can be scored before slicing to add a special touch. To score, make a lengthwise groove in the fruit with a citrus stripper. Continue to make grooves ¼ to ½ inch apart until the entire fruit has been grooved.*

Combine wine, cranberry juice cocktail, orange juice, liqueur, orange slices and lime slices in large glass pitcher. Chill 2 to 8 hours before serving.

Pour into glasses; add orange and/or lime slices from sangría to each glass. *Makes about 7 cups, 10 to 12 servings*

Sparkling Sangría: Just before serving, tilt pitcher and slowly add 2 cups well-chilled sparkling water or club soda. Pour into glasses; add orange and/or lime slices from sangría to each glass. Makes about 9 cups, or 12 to 15 servings.

Icy Fruit Tea

CONCENTRATE

- **4 tea bags**
- **1 cup boiling water**
- **½ cup honey**
- **¼ cup crushed packed fresh mint leaves**
- **1 cup orange juice**
- **¾ cup pineapple juice**
- **¼ cup fresh lime juice**

MIXER

- **Ice cubes**
- **1½ quarts carbonated water**

For concentrate, place tea bags in medium bowl. Add boiling water and steep 10 minutes. Remove tea bags. Add honey and mint; mix well. Mix fruit juices in 1-quart container. Add tea mixture and refrigerate until ready to use.

For tea, fill 12-ounce glass with ice cubes. Add ½ cup tea concentrate and fill glass with carbonated water.

Makes 6 servings

Tip: Garnish with a pineapple spear and mint sprig.

Favorite recipe from **National Honey Board**

Cranberry Sangria

Orange Iced Tea

2 SUNKIST® oranges
4 cups boiling water
5 tea bags
Ice cubes
Honey or brown sugar to taste

With vegetable peeler, peel each orange in continuous spiral, removing only outer colored layer of peel (eat peeled fruit or save for other uses). In large pitcher, pour boiling water over tea bags and orange peel. Cover and steep 5 minutes. Remove tea bags; chill tea mixture with peel in covered container. To serve, remove peel and pour over ice cubes in tall glasses. Sweeten to taste with honey. Garnish with orange quarter-cartwheel slices and fresh mint leaves, if desired.

Makes 4 (8-ounce) servings

Lemon Herbal Iced Tea

2 SUNKIST® lemons
4 cups boiling water
6 herbal tea bags (peppermint and spearmint blend or ginger-flavored)
Ice cubes
Honey or sugar to taste

With vegetable peeler, peel each lemon in continuous spiral, removing only outer colored layer of peel (save peeled fruit for other uses). In large pitcher, pour boiling water over tea bags and lemon peel. Cover and steep 10 minutes. Remove tea bags; chill tea mixture with peel in covered container. To serve, remove peel and pour over ice cubes in tall glasses. Sweeten to taste with honey. Garnish with lemon half-cartwheel slices, if desired.

Makes 4 (8-ounce) servings

The color and flavor of honey is determined by the type of flower from which the nectar originated. The color of honey ranges form pale gold to deep amber. In general, the lighter the color the milder the flavor.

Orange Iced Tea and Lemon Herbal Iced Tea

Caribbean Dream

¾ cup vanilla ice cream
¾ cup pineapple sherbet
¾ cup tropical fruit salad, drained
¼ cup frozen banana-orange juice concentrate
¼ teaspoon rum-flavored extract

1. Place ice cream, sherbet, fruit salad, concentrate and extract in blender. Blend on medium speed 1 to 2 minutes or until smooth and well blended.

2. Pour into 2 serving glasses. Serve immediately.

Makes 2 servings

Serve It With Style: Try adding a tablespoon of rum instead of rum-flavored extract for a more mature flavor.

Lighten Up: To reduce the fat, replace vanilla ice cream with reduced-fat or fat-free ice cream or frozen yogurt.

Prep time: 10 minutes

Cool Strawberry Drink

1 fresh pineapple
1 cup fresh strawberries, hulled and halved
2 teaspoons sugar
1 pint lemon sherbet
4 cups chilled lemon-lime beverage or ginger ale

To prepare pineapple, cut off both ends. Remove rind and eyes with sharp knife. Cut pineapple into lengthwise quarters. Remove core; cut fruit into chunks. Measure 1 cup pineapple; refrigerate remaining pineapple for another use. Place 1 cup pineapple and strawberries in a large bowl; sprinkle with sugar. Let stand until ready to use. Divide fruit among four large glasses; add ½ cup sherbet to each glass. Pour 1 cup lemon-lime beverage into each glass. Serve immediately.

Makes 4 servings

Caribbean Dream

Sangrita

3 cups DEL MONTE® Tomato Juice
1½ cups orange juice
½ cup salsa
Juice of 1 medium lime

1. Mix all ingredients in large pitcher; chill.
2. Serve over ice with fruit garnishes, if desired.

Makes 6 (6-ounce) servings

Prep Time: 3 minutes

Snappy Cooler

3 to 6 ounces SNAP-E-TOM® Tomato and Chile Cocktail, chilled
3 ounces orange juice, chilled

1. Combine ingredients. Serve over ice, if desired.

Makes 1 serving

Prep Time: 2 minutes

Peach-Lemon Frost

3 fresh California peaches, peeled, halved, pitted and quartered
1 cup 2% low-fat milk
½ cup fresh lemon juice
3 ice cubes, crushed
2 teaspoons grated lemon peel
½ pint vanilla ice milk

Add peaches to food processor or blender. Process until smooth to measure 2 cups. Add low-fat milk, lemon juice, ice cubes and lemon peel. Process until smooth. Continue processing at low speed; slowly add ice milk until well blended. Pour into glasses. Serve immediately. *Makes 4 servings*

Favorite recipe from **California Tree Fruit Agreement**

Sangrita

Mango Batido

1 large mango
1¾ cups fat-free (skim) milk
2 tablespoons frozen orange-peach-mango juice concentrate
4 ice cubes
⅛ teaspoon almond extract (optional)

1. Peel mango. Cut fruit away from pit; cut fruit into cubes.

2. Combine all ingredients in blender; blend until smooth. Serve immediately.

Makes 4 servings

Tip: Chill mango before preparing recipe.

Choco-Berry Cooler

¾ cup cold milk
¼ cup sliced fresh strawberries
2 tablespoons HERSHEY'S® Syrup
2 tablespoons plus 2 small scoops vanilla ice cream, divided
Cold ginger ale or club soda
Fresh strawberry
Mint leaves (optional)

1. Place milk, strawberries, chocolate syrup and 2 tablespoons ice cream in blender container. Cover and blend until smooth.

2. Alternate remaining 2 scoops of ice cream and chocolate mixture in tall ice soda cream glass; fill glass with ginger ale. Garnish with a fresh strawberry and mint leaves, if desired. Serve immediately.

Makes one 14-ounce serving

Variations: Before blending, substitute one of the following fruits for fresh strawberries: 3 tablespoons frozen strawberries with syrup, thawed; ½ peeled fresh peach *or* ⅓ cup canned peach slices; 2 slices canned *or* ¼ cup canned crushed pineapple; ¼ cup sweetened fresh raspberries *or* 3 tablespoons frozen raspberries with syrup, thawed.

Mango Batido

Sunny Citrus Float

- **½ cup sweetened lemon-flavored iced tea mix**
- **1 quart water**
- **⅓ cup (3 ounces) frozen lemonade concentrate, thawed**
- **⅓ can (3 ounces) frozen orange juice concentrate, thawed**
- **Vanilla frozen yougurt**

Combine all ingredients except frozen yogurt in large pitcher. To serve, fill glasses about ⅔ full with iced tea mixture. Top each glass with 1 scoop frozen yogurt. *Makes 4 to 6 servings*

Cardamom-Spiked Fresh Lemonade Spritzer

- **40 whole white cardamom pods, cracked**
- **1¼ cups sugar**
- **3 cups water**
- **2 cups fresh lemon juice**
- **1 bottle (750 ml) Asti Spumante or club soda**
- **Additional sugar (optional)**
- **Ice**
- **Mint leaves for garnish**

Combine cardamom pods with 1¼ cups sugar and water in medium saucepan. Cook and stir over high heat until mixture comes to a boil and sugar dissolves. Reduce heat to low; cover and simmer 30 minutes. Remove from heat; cool completely. Refrigerate 2 hours or up to 3 days.

Pour mixture through strainer into 3-quart pitcher; discard pods. Stir in lemon juice and Asti Spumante. Stir in additional sugar to taste. Serve over ice. Garnish, if desired. *Makes 6 servings*

Cardamom imparts a sweet and spicy Indian flavor to recipes. It is a member of the ginger family and is often found blended with other spices to make Curry powder.

Sunny Citrus Float

Acknowledgments

The publisher would like to thank the companies and organizations listed below for the use of their recipes and photographs in this publication.

BelGioioso® Cheese, Inc.

Bob Evans®

California Tree Fruit Agreement

Chef Paul Prudhomme's Magic Seasoning Blends®

ConAgra Foods®

Del Monte Corporation

Dole Food Company, Inc.

Florida's Citrus Growers

Guiltless Gourmet®

Hershey Foods Corporation

The Hidden Valley® Food Products Company

Hillshire Farm®

Kahlúa® Liqueur

The Kingsford Products Company

Lawry's® Foods

Lee Kum Kee (USA) Inc.

McIlhenny Company (TABASCO® brand Pepper Sauce)

Minnesota Cultivated Wild Rice Council

National Chicken Council / US Poultry & Egg Association

National Honey Board

National Pork Board

National Turkey Federation

NatraTaste® is a registered trademark of Stadt Corporation

Reckitt Benckiser Inc.

The J.M. Smucker Company

The Sugar Association, Inc.

Property of © 2003 Sunkist Growers, Inc. All rights reserved

Unilever Bestfoods North America

Wisconsin Milk Marketing Board

Index

Notes

METRIC CONVERSION CHART

VOLUME MEASUREMENTS (dry)

1/8 teaspoon = 0.5 mL
1/4 teaspoon = 1 mL
1/2 teaspoon = 2 mL
3/4 teaspoon = 4 mL
1 teaspoon = 5 mL
1 tablespoon = 15 mL
2 tablespoons = 30 mL
1/4 cup = 60 mL
1/3 cup = 75 mL
1/2 cup = 125 mL
2/3 cup = 150 mL
3/4 cup = 175 mL
1 cup = 250 mL
2 cups = 1 pint = 500 mL
3 cups = 750 mL
4 cups = 1 quart = 1 L

VOLUME MEASUREMENTS (fluid)

1 fluid ounce (2 tablespoons) = 30 mL
4 fluid ounces (1/2 cup) = 125 mL
8 fluid ounces (1 cup) = 250 mL
12 fluid ounces (1 1/2 cups) = 375 mL
16 fluid ounces (2 cups) = 500 mL

WEIGHTS (mass)

1/2 ounce = 15 g
1 ounce = 30 g
3 ounces = 90 g
4 ounces = 120 g
8 ounces = 225 g
10 ounces = 285 g
12 ounces = 360 g
16 ounces = 1 pound = 450 g

DIMENSIONS

1/16 inch = 2 mm
1/8 inch = 3 mm
1/4 inch = 6 mm
1/2 inch = 1.5 cm
3/4 inch = 2 cm
1 inch = 2.5 cm

OVEN TEMPERATURES

250°F = 120°C
275°F = 140°C
300°F = 150°C
325°F = 160°C
350°F = 180°C
375°F = 190°C
400°F = 200°C
425°F = 220°C
450°F = 230°C

BAKING PAN SIZES

Utensil	Size in Inches/Quarts	Metric Volume	Size in Centimeters
Baking or Cake Pan (square or rectangular)	8×8×2	2 L	20×20×5
	9×9×2	2.5 L	23×23×5
	12×8×2	3 L	30×20×5
	13×9×2	3.5 L	33×23×5
Loaf Pan	8×4×3	1.5 L	20×10×7
	9×5×3	2 L	23×13×7
Round Layer Cake Pan	8×1½	1.2 L	20×4
	9×1½	1.5 L	23×4
Pie Plate	8×1¼	750 mL	20×3
	9×1¼	1 L	23×3
Baking Dish or Casserole	1 quart	1 L	—
	1½ quart	1.5 L	—
	2 quart	2 L	—